Large Print Adult Coloring Book:

Owls & Other Birds

Big, beautiful & fanciful bird designs

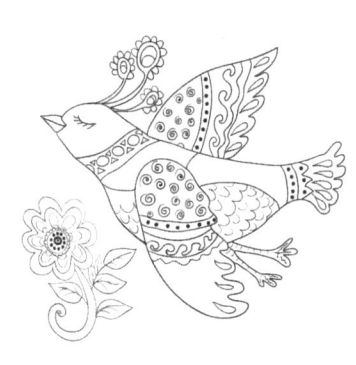 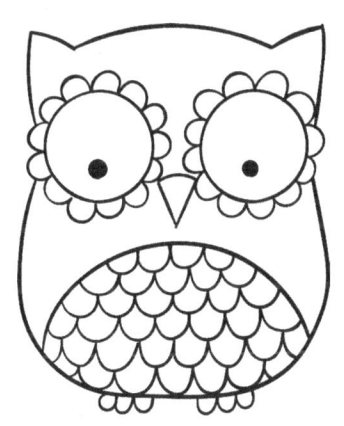 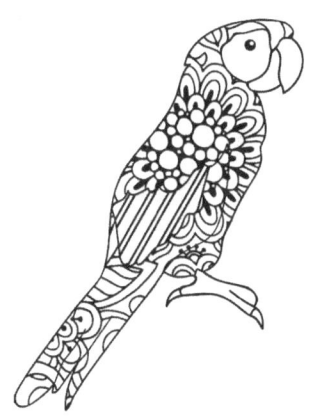

A relaxing large-print coloring book for adults
featuring 48 beautiful pictures of
simple and decorative owl and other bird designs

BRILLIANT ACTIVITY BOOKS

BRILLIANTACTIVITYBOOKS.COM & MYRIA.COM/SHOP

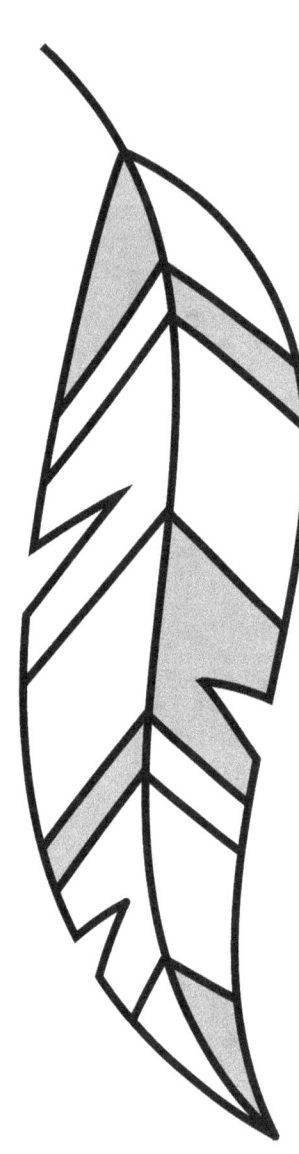

A few other books you might like...

- *Large Print Adult Coloring Book: Big, Beautiful & Simple Designs,* and *Big, Beautiful & Simple Flowers* and *Big, Beautiful & Simple Mandalas* (companions to this book)
- *Motivation & Mandalas Adult Coloring Book*
- *Large Print Word Search Puzzles* (2 volumes)
- Large Print Address Books (3 volumes: Birds & Flowers; Pinstripes; Flowers)
- *Vintage Women* Coloring Books - Featuring dozens of fashions from the past
- *Something Old: Vintage Wedding Dress Fashion Look Book*
- Myria's blank recipe books (5 volumes: Family recipes, Dinners, Desserts, Slow Cooker, Gluten-Free)

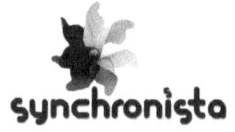

synchronista

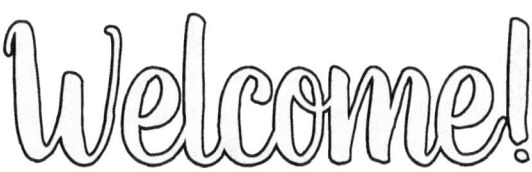

Welcome!

Inside are 48 letter-size pages — each one with a big, beautiful and relaxing image to color. We have tried to offer you many different ways to enjoy the benefits of both simplicity *and* creativity.

To that end, the areas to color are larger than those found in many other adult coloring books. Some pages offer more complexity than others, but all of the designs have dark lines and plenty of space to color without the need for super-fine markers or pens.

These simpler versions of patterns and hand-drawn decorative designs have been chosen especially for those new to the world of adult coloring books, anyone who doesn't want to color in complicated drawings, and those with vision or motor issues for whom less-intricate artwork is preferable.

Although relaxation and fun both come from the coloring process itself, when you finish each page, you will be left with the lasting reward of a beautiful piece of art!

A few quick notes...

- Each coloring activity is printed on only one side of the page. While many people have reported excellent results using colored pencils on designs like these, if you use pens or markers, you may want to slip a blank sheet of paper (one at the end of the book) behind the page as you color to avoid bleed-through. Pages 6 & 7 offer space to test your coloring medium of choice.

- The coloring pages themselves do not have page numbers visible on the front. To navigate using the index, found on the following two pages, please reference the numbers opposite each picture.

- Don't miss the free cut-out bookmarks at the back of the book (page 105).

- If you liked this coloring book, a review on Amazon would be greatly appreciated. Thank you for supporting independent publishers!

Large print coloring book

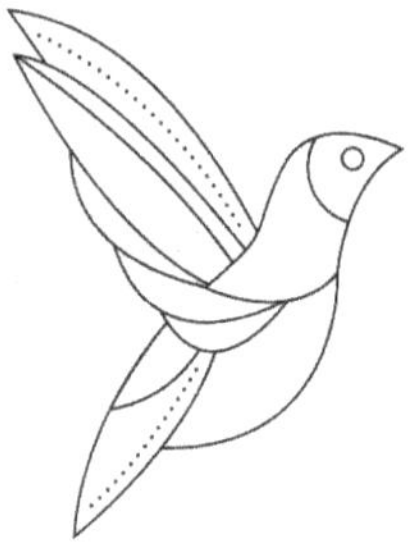

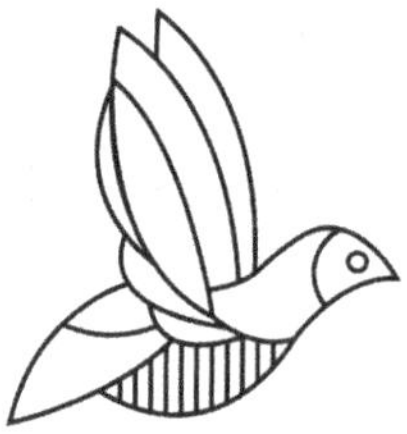

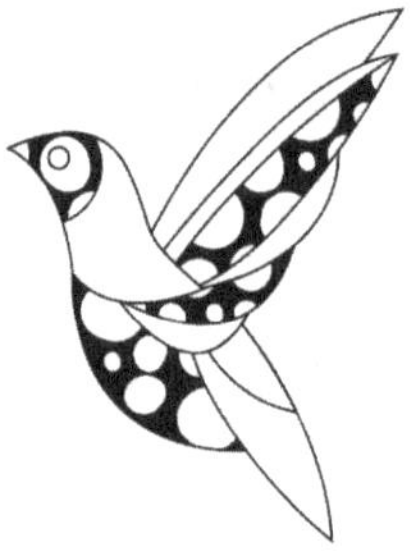

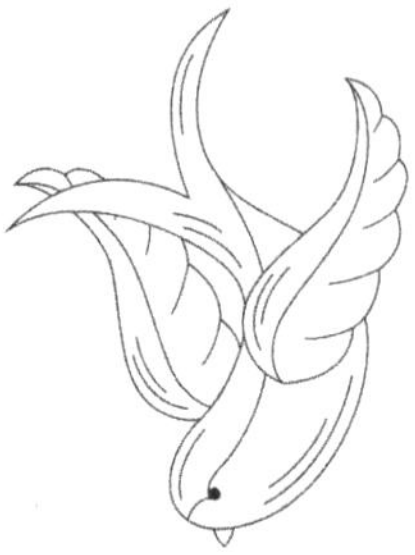

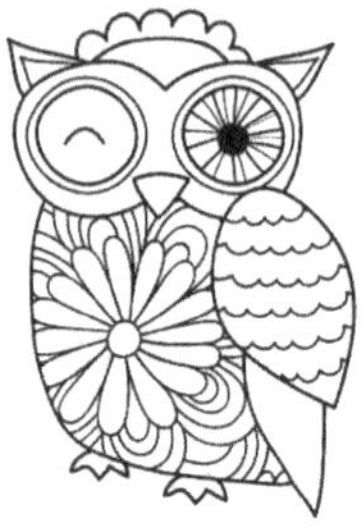

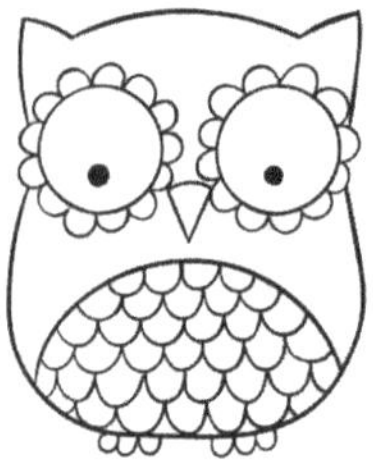

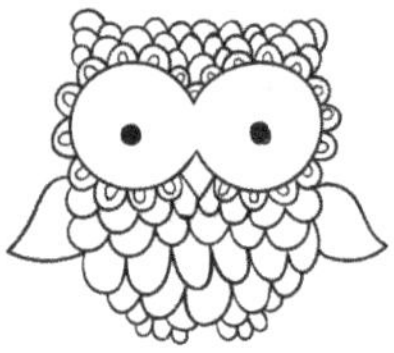

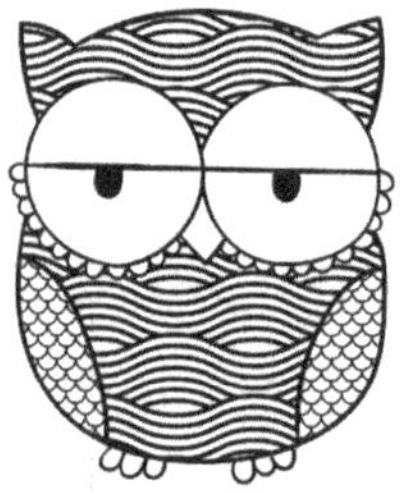

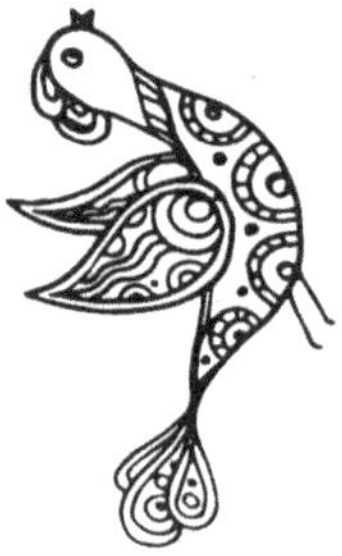

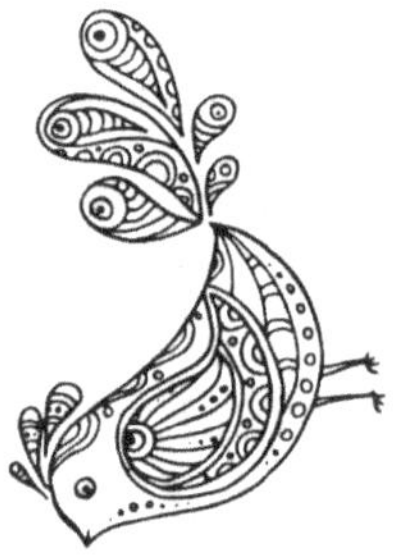

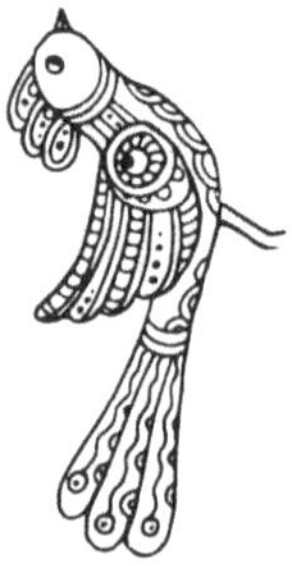

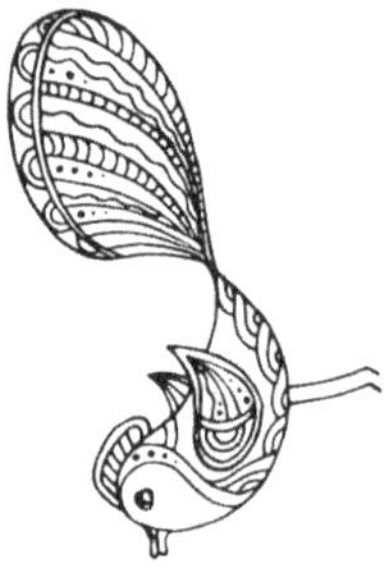

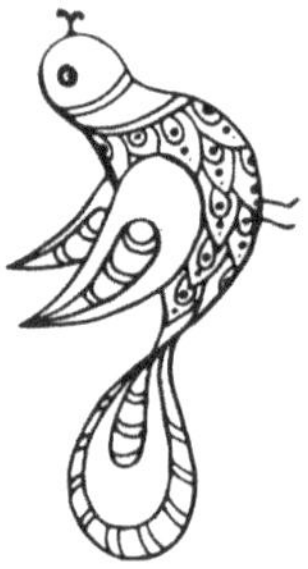

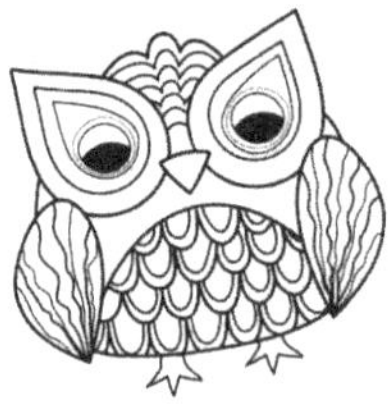

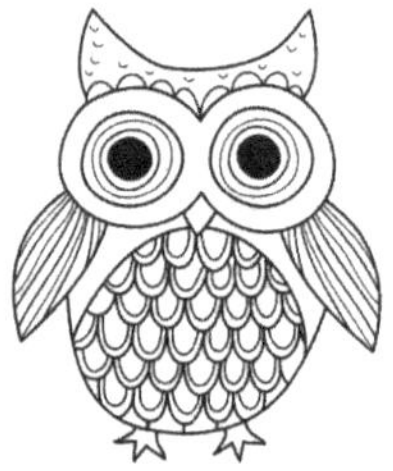

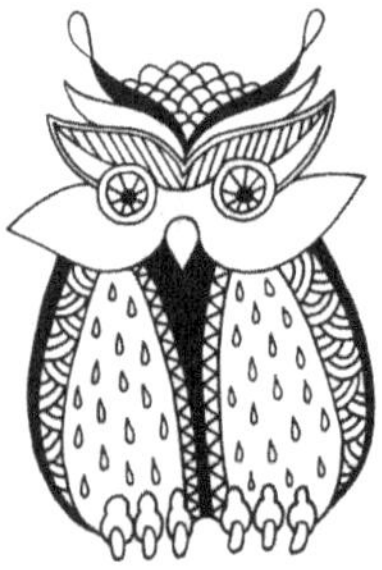

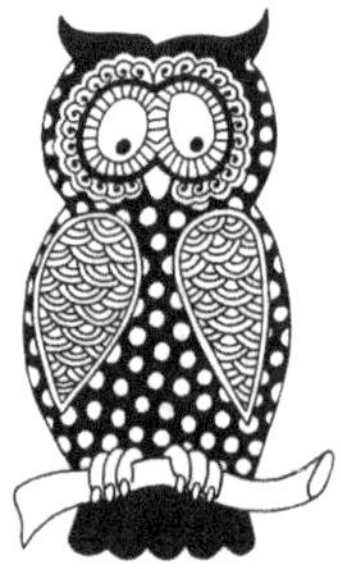

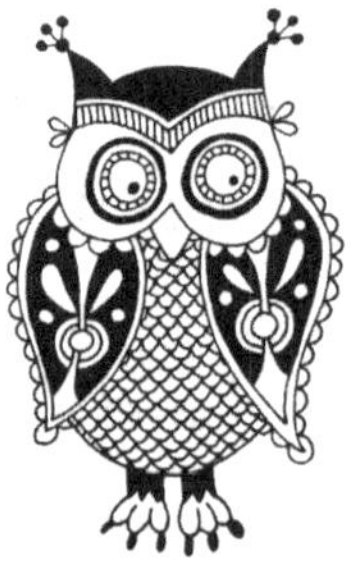

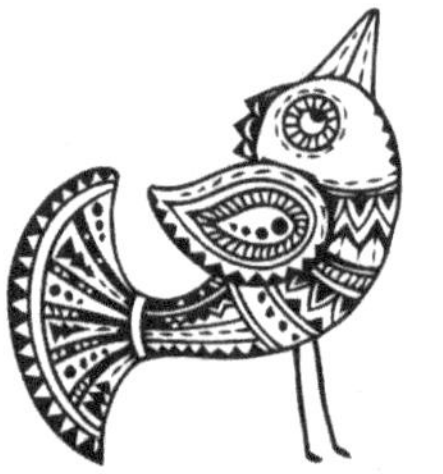

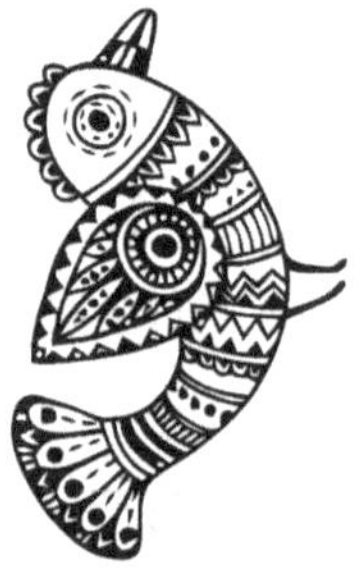

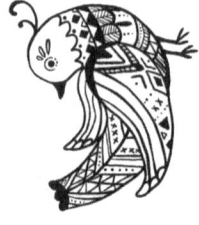 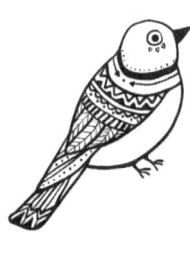 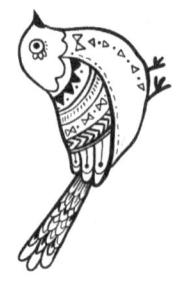 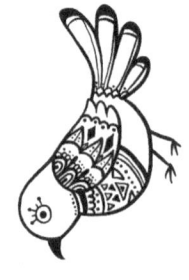 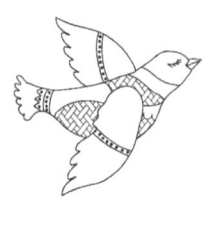

Owls and birds page index

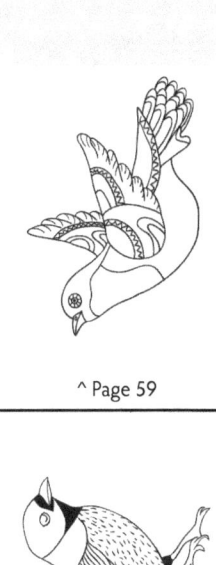

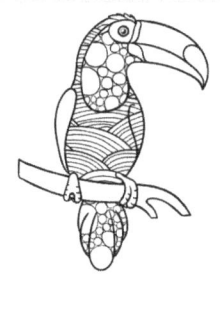

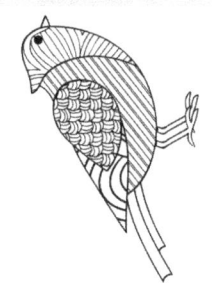

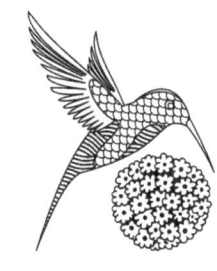

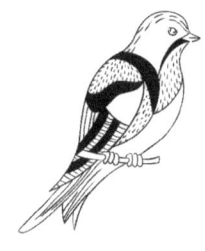

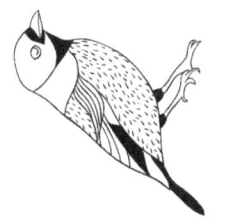

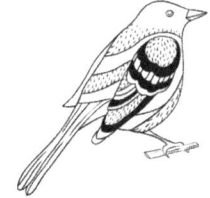

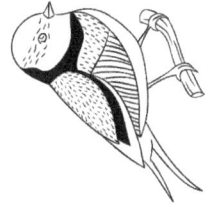

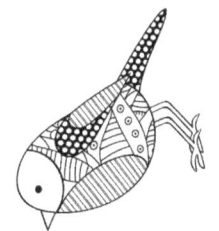

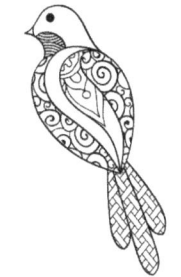

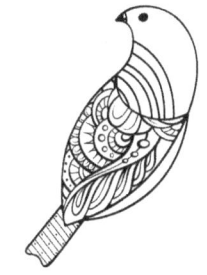

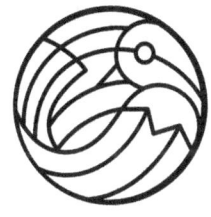

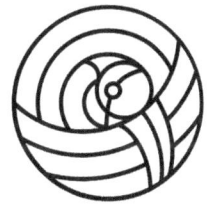

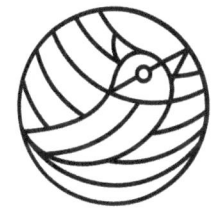

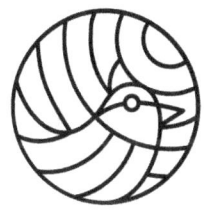

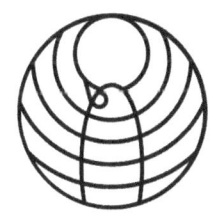

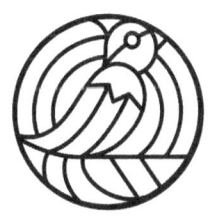

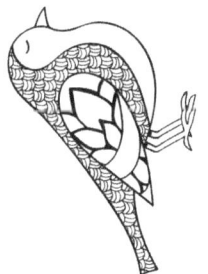

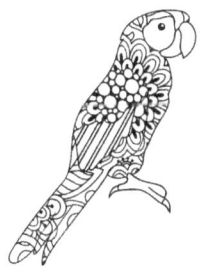

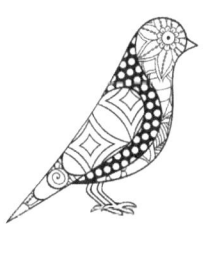

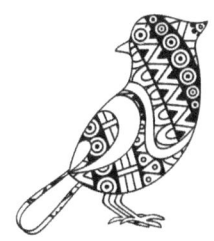

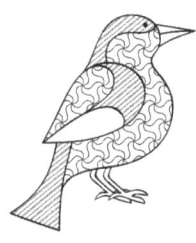

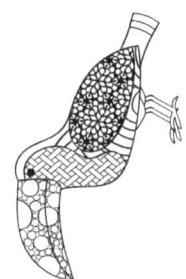

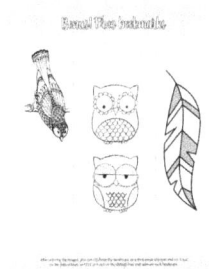

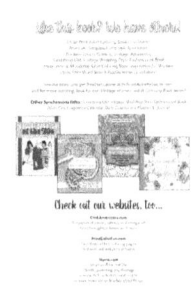

The above image is from our book, *Large Print Adult Flowers Coloring Book: Big, Beautiful & Simple Flowers*

Color & medium testing pages

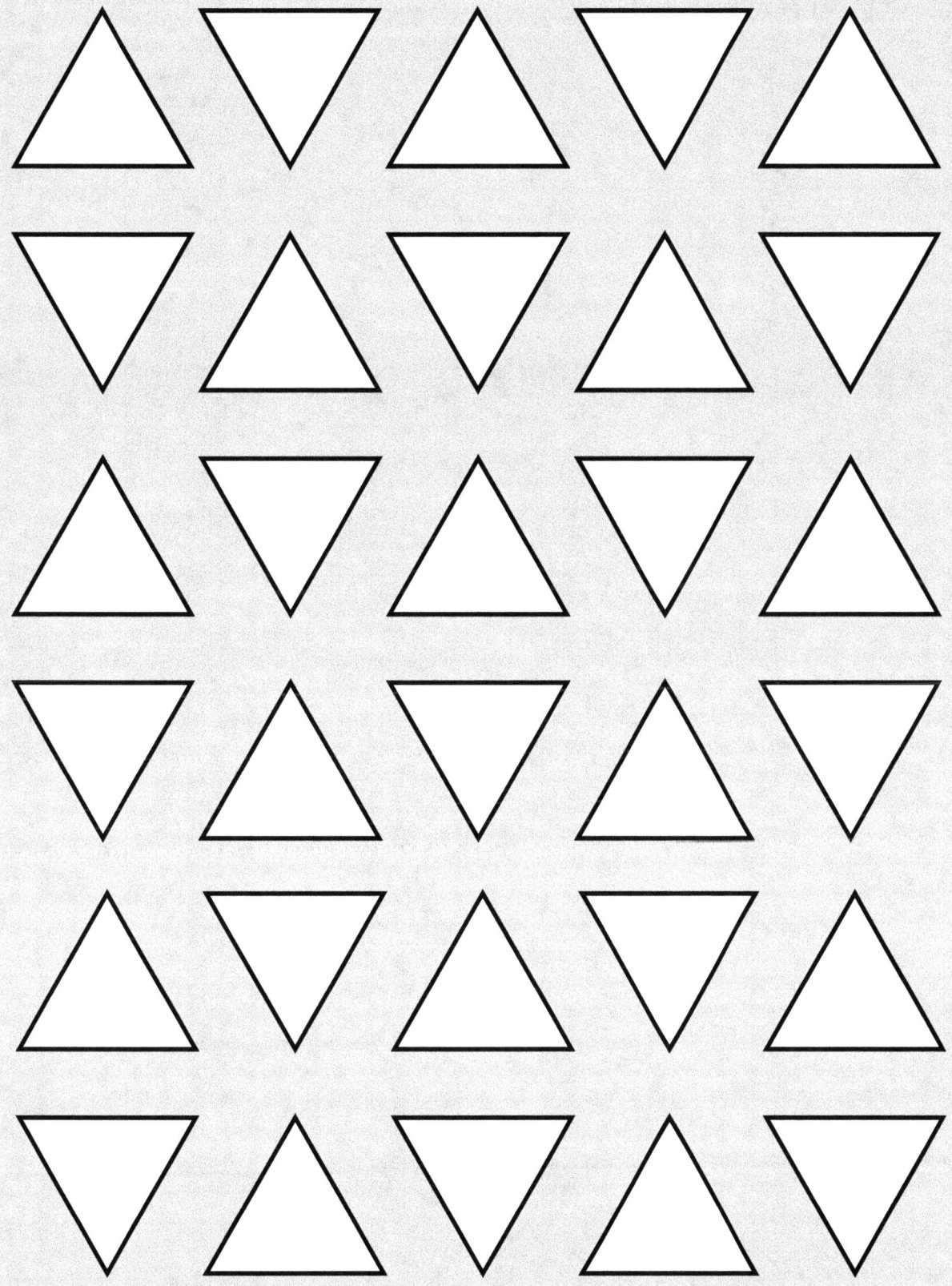

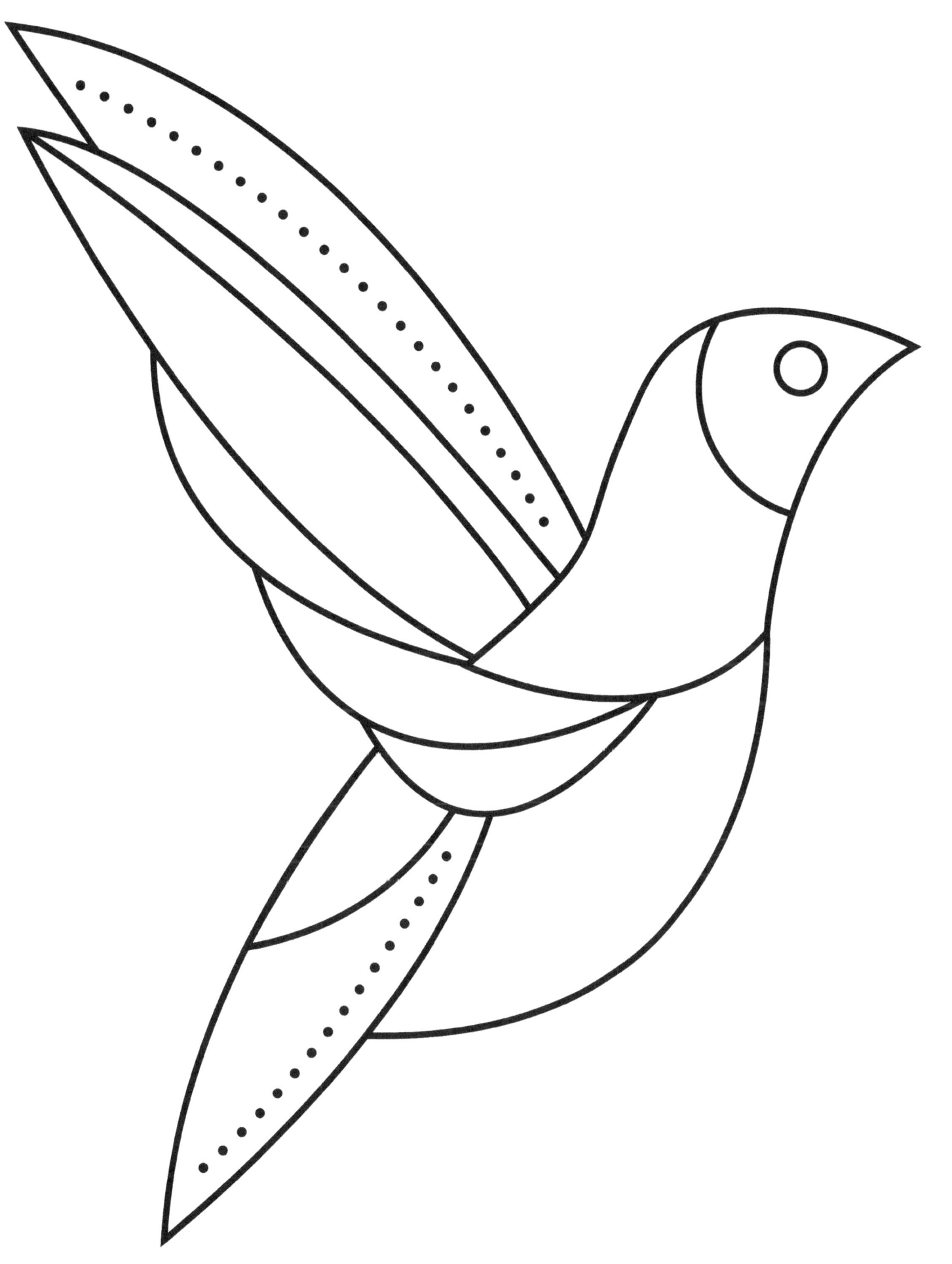

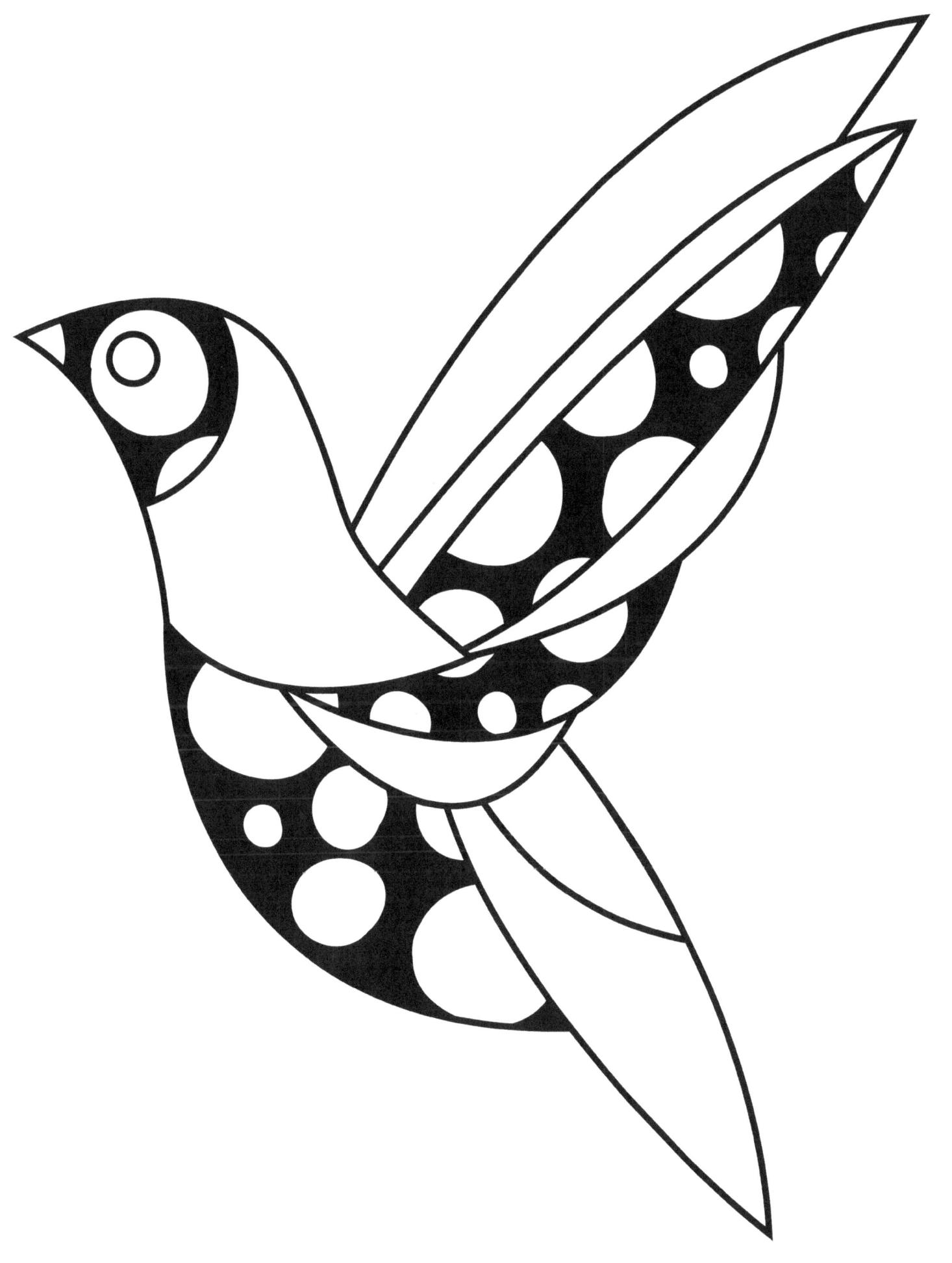

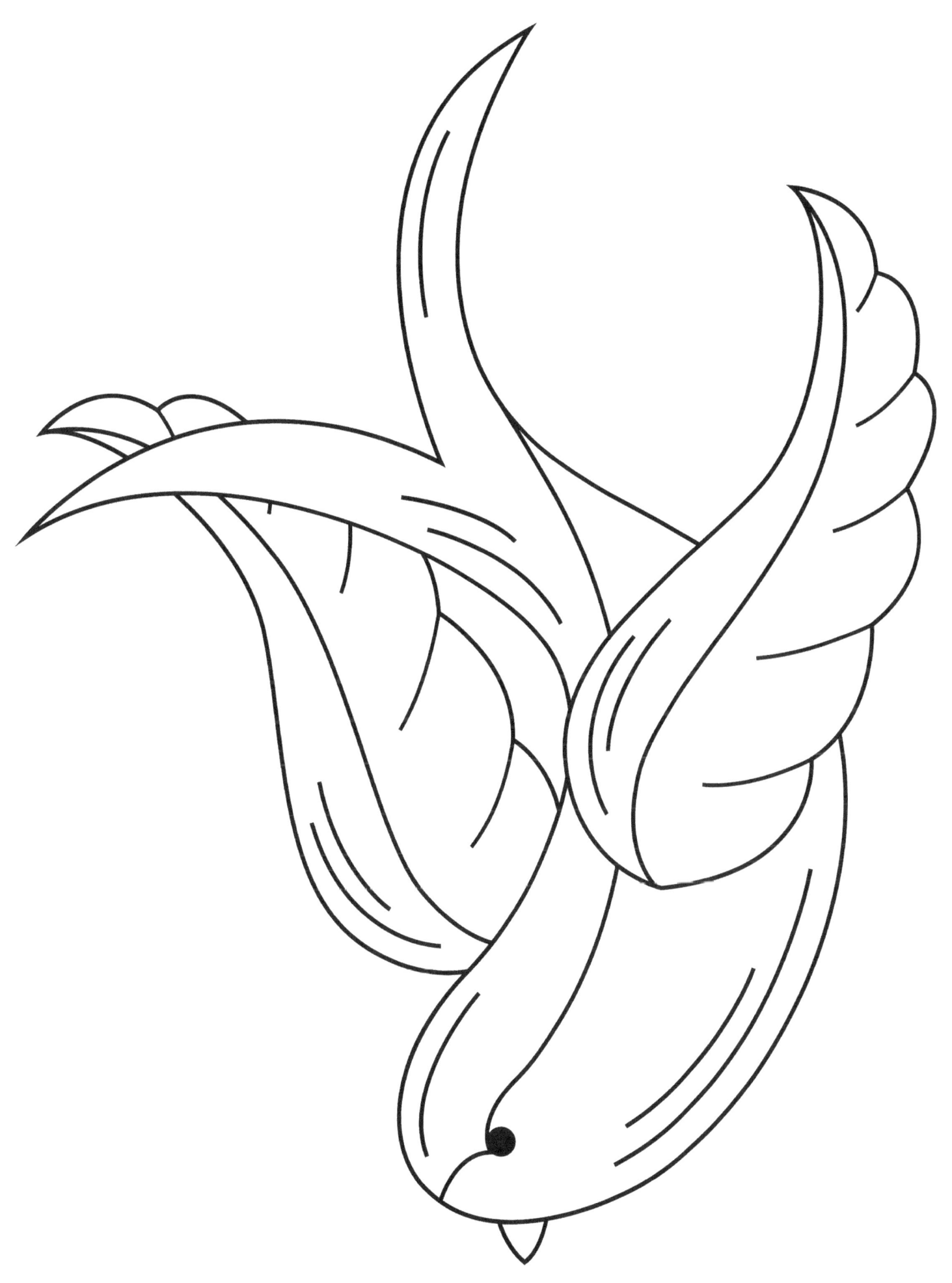

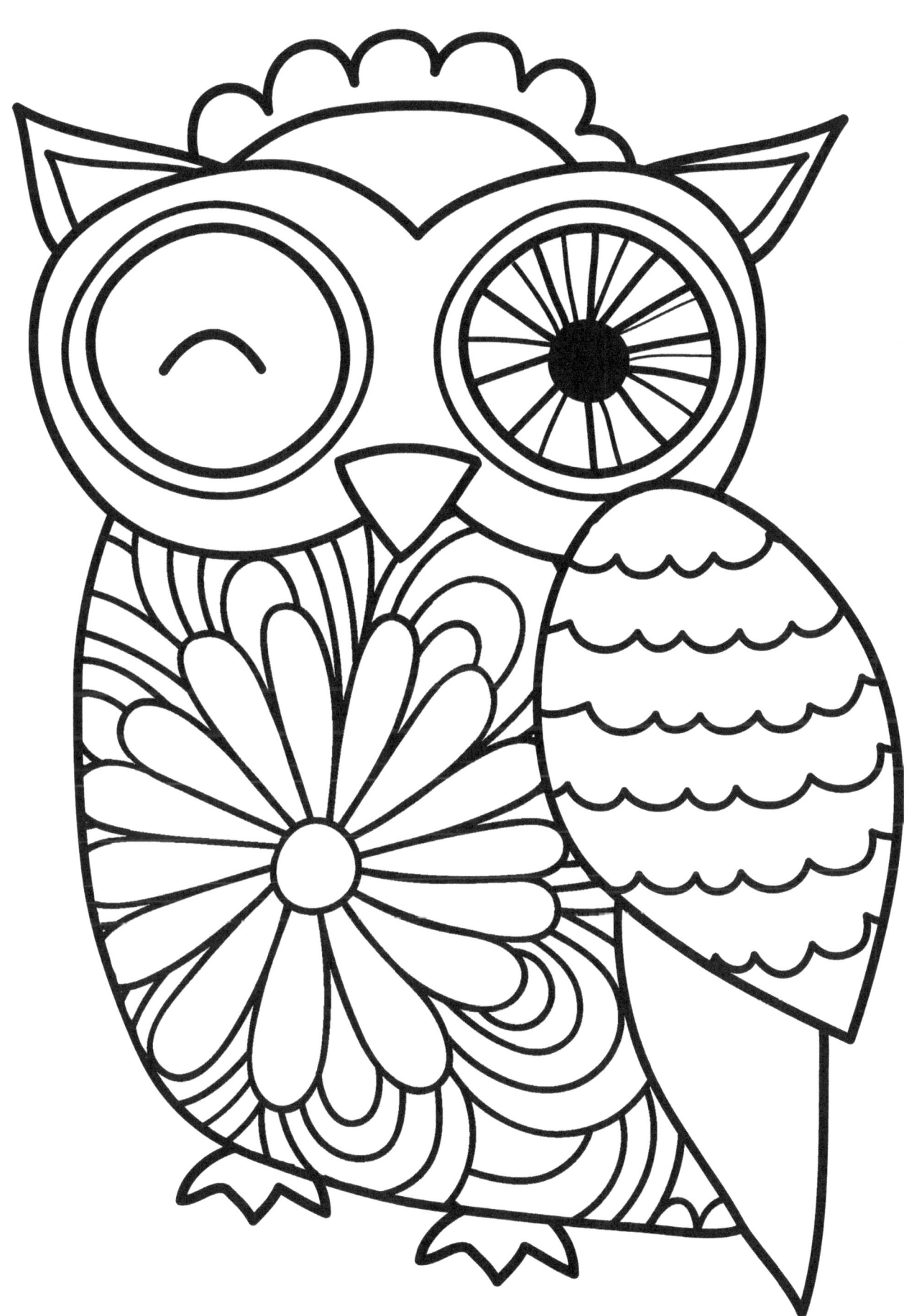

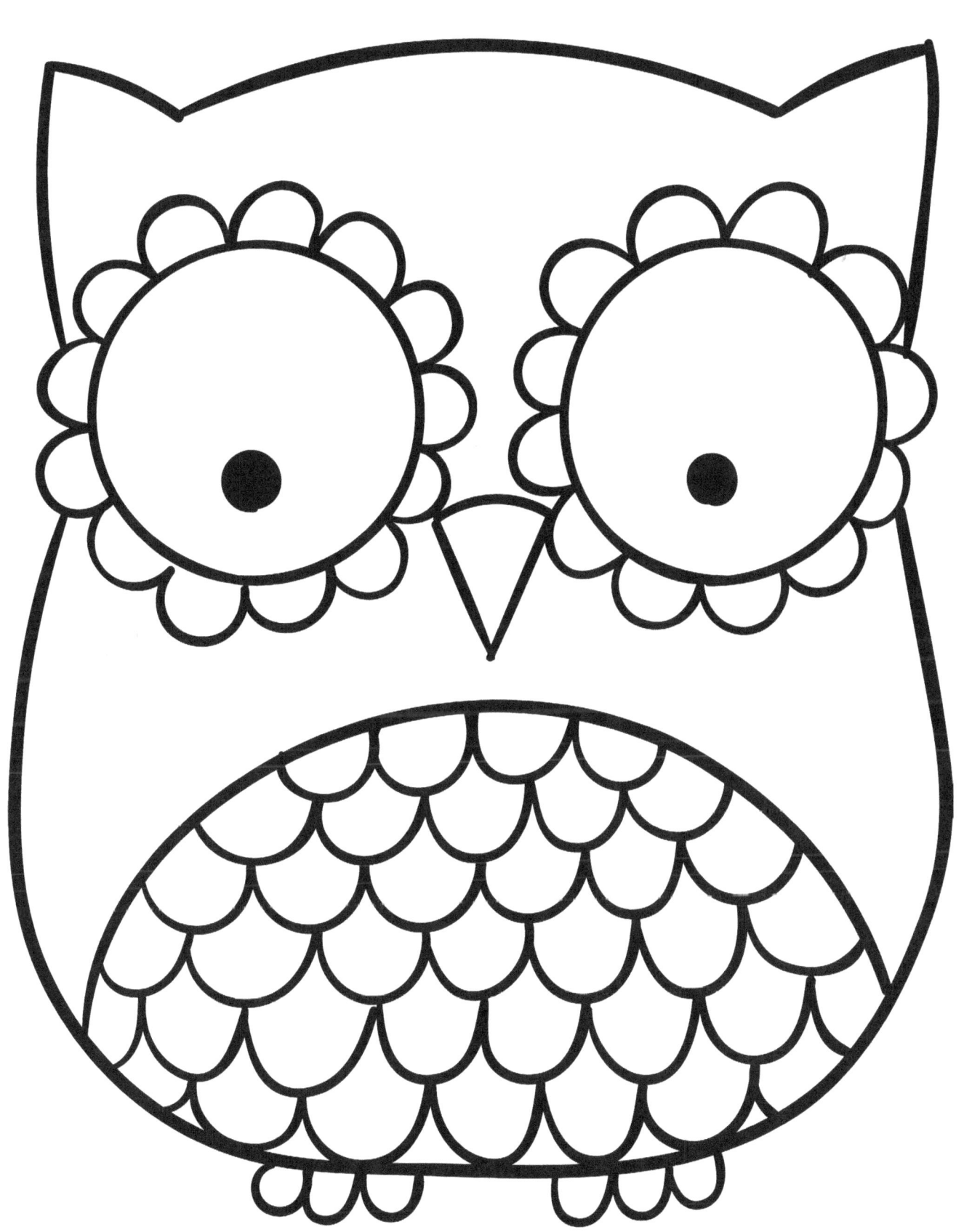

Large Print Adult Coloring Book: Owls and Other Birds

Large Print Adult Coloring Book: Owls and Other Birds

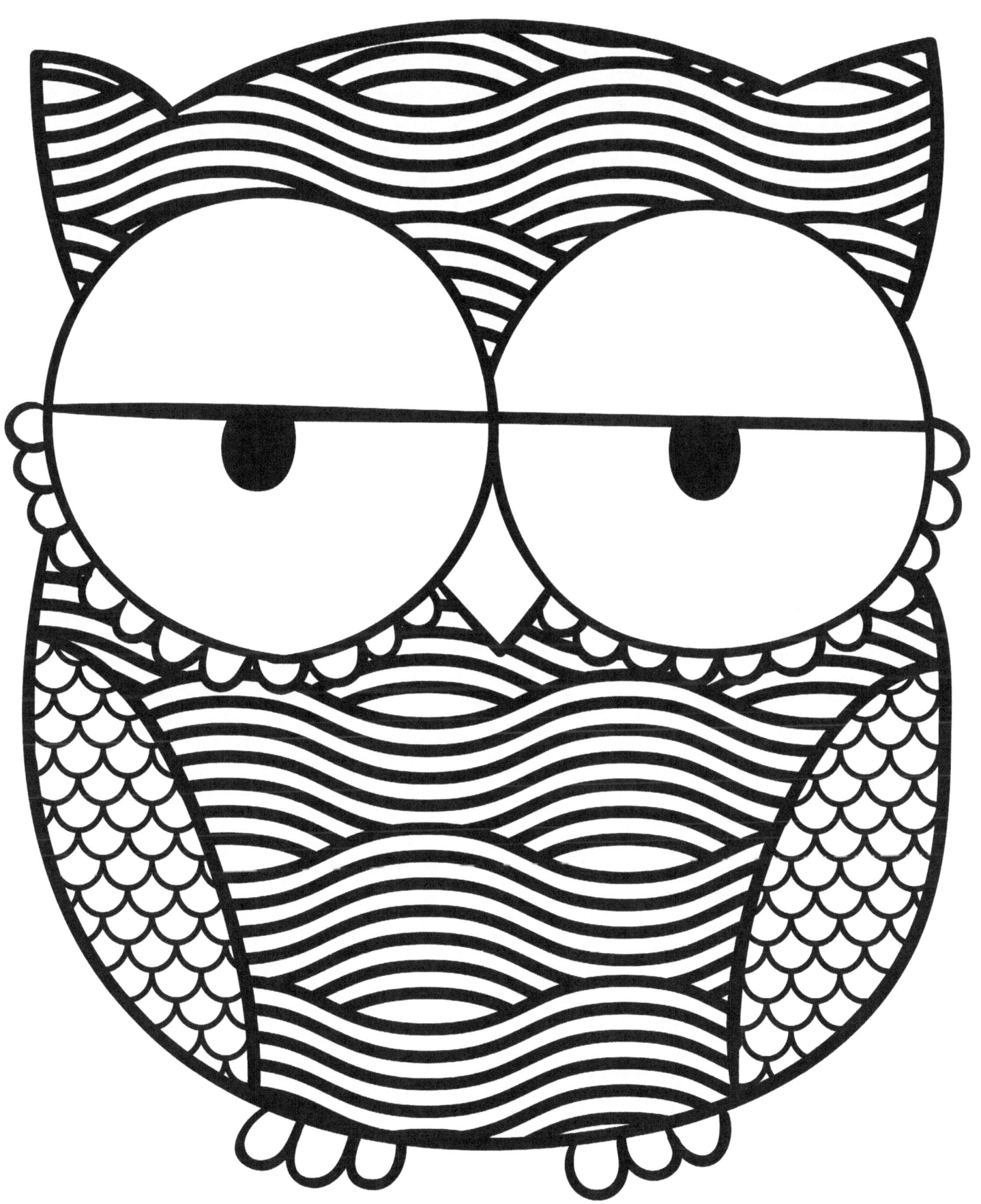

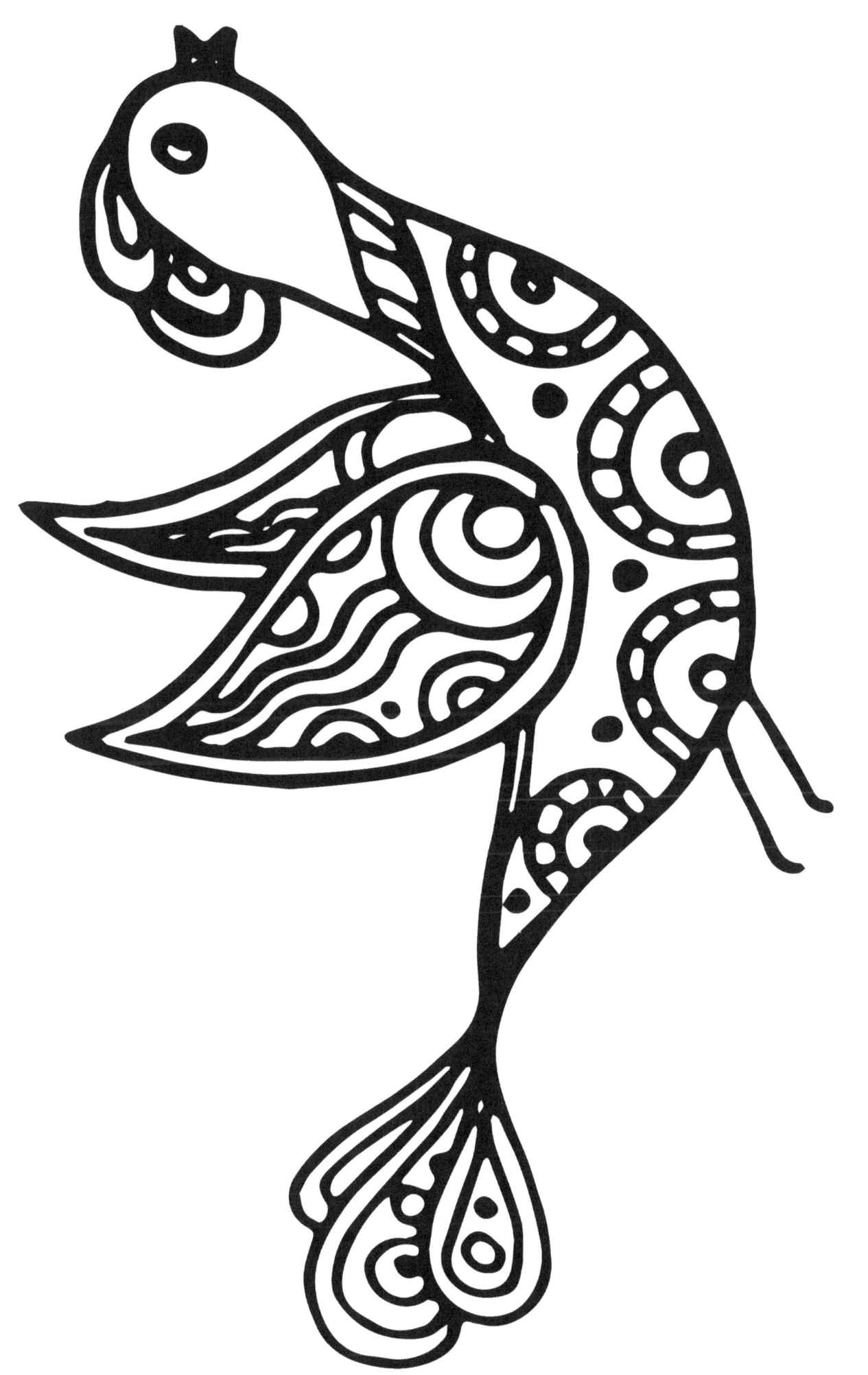

Large Print Adult Coloring Book: Owls and Other Birds

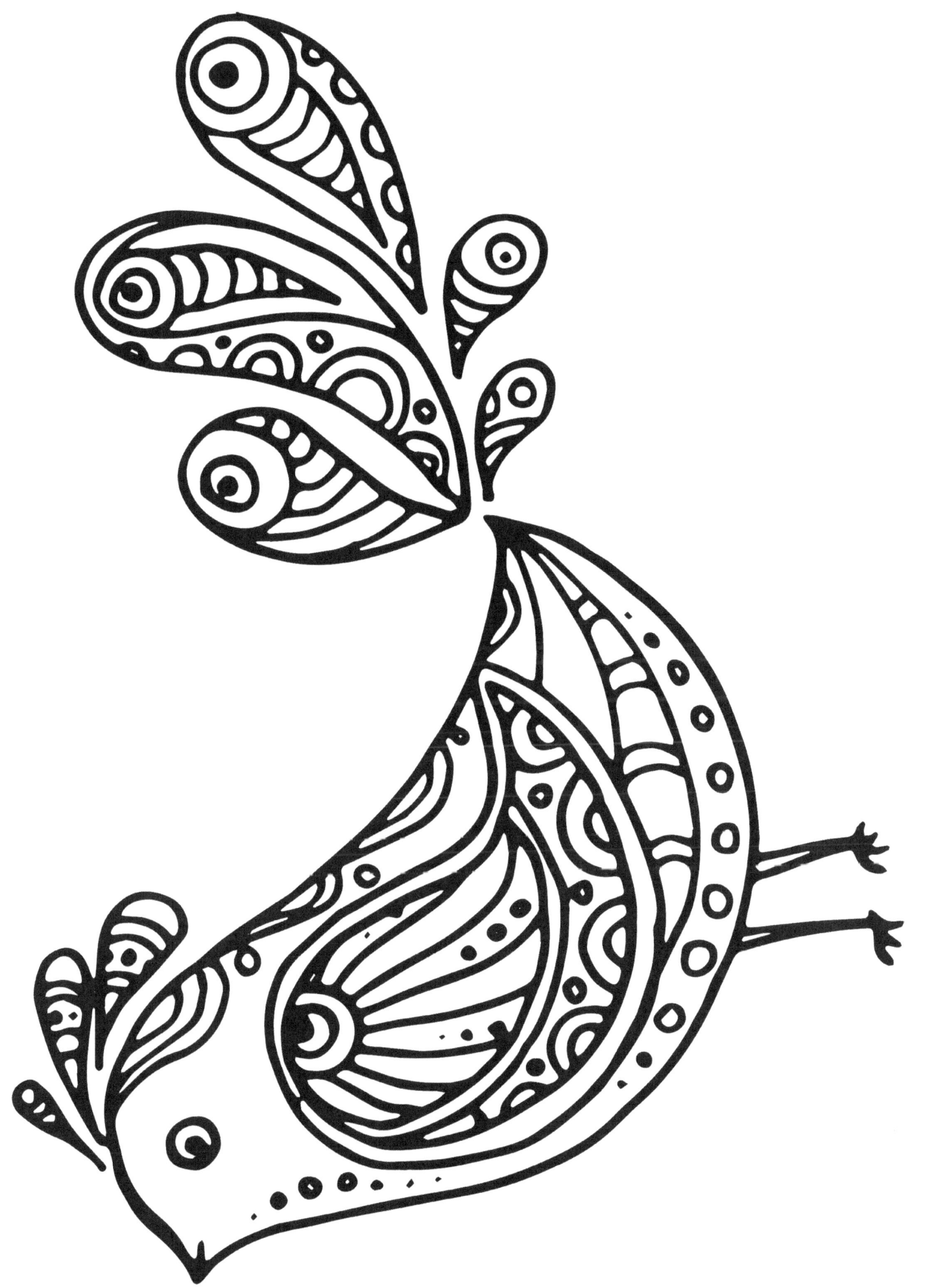

Large Print Adult Coloring Book: Owls and Other Birds

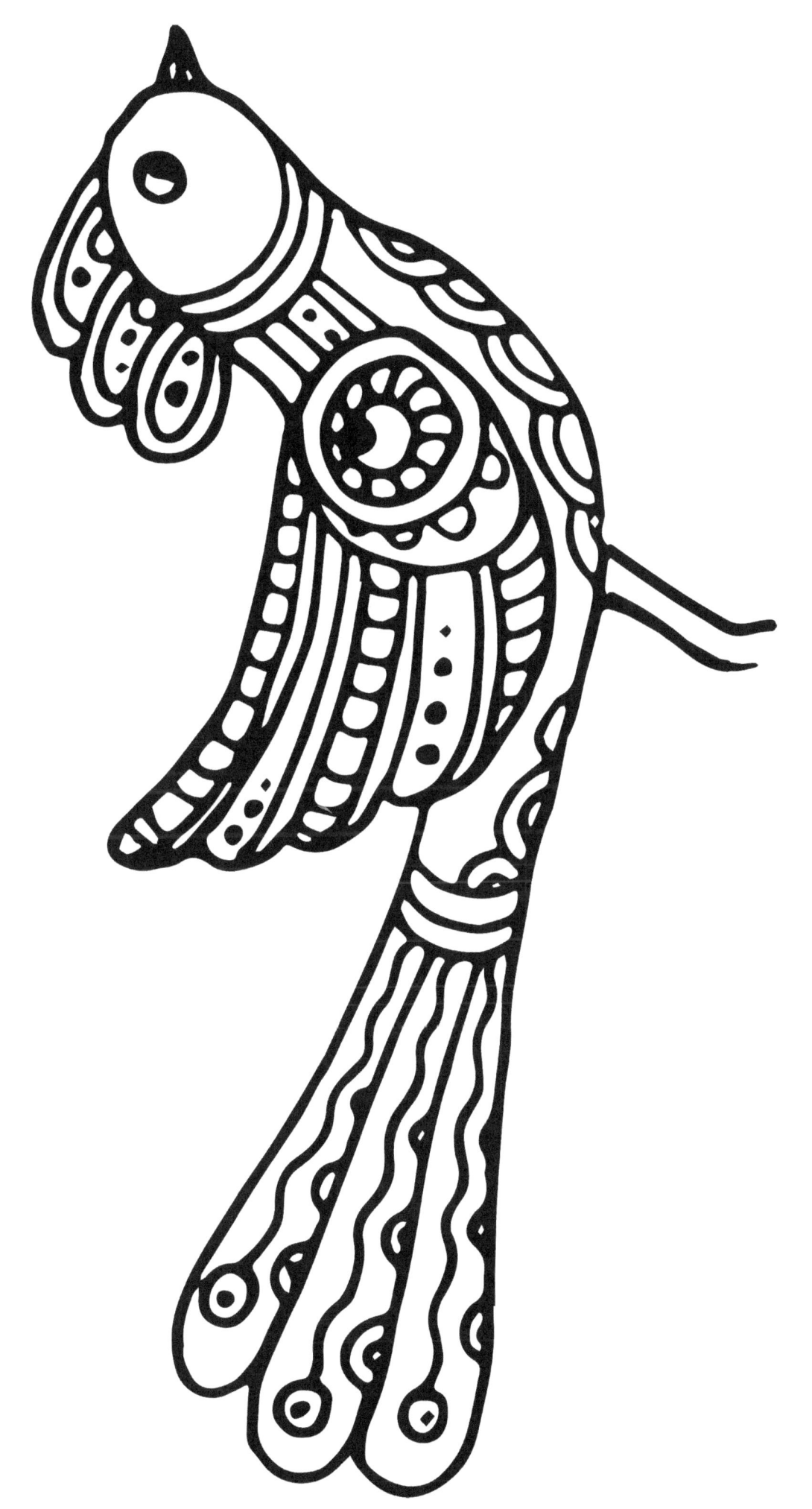

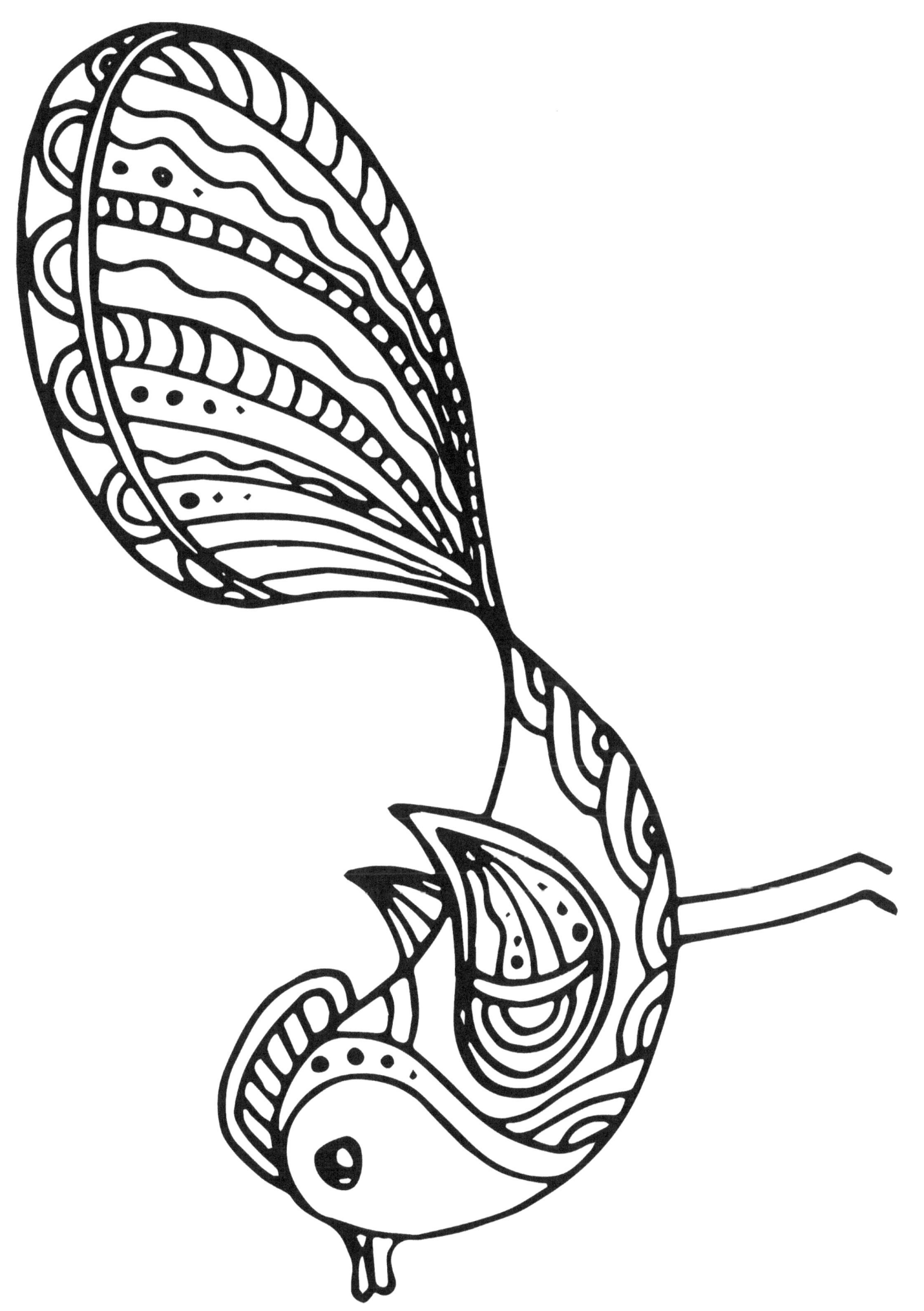

Large Print Adult Coloring Book: Owls and Other Birds

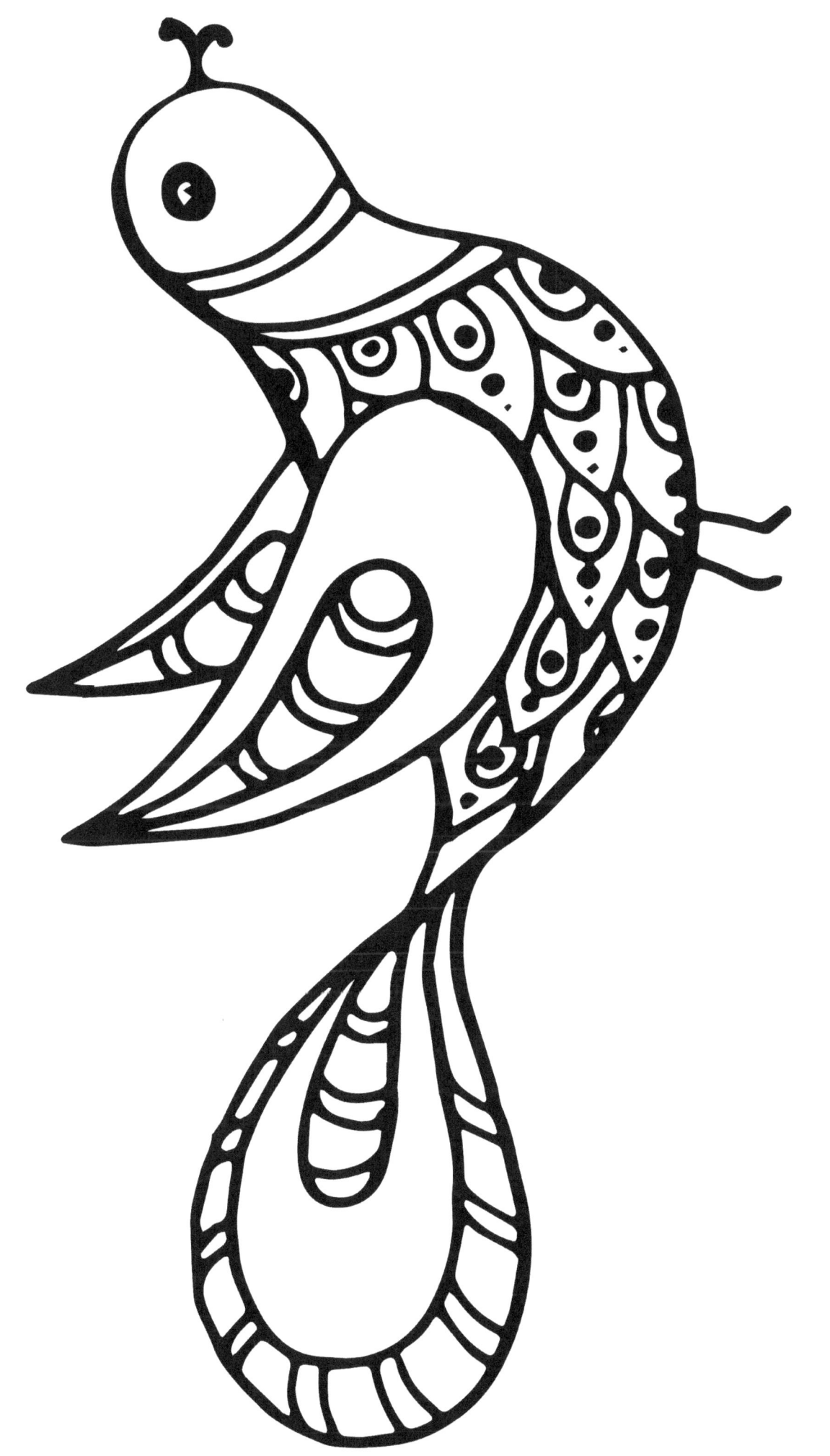

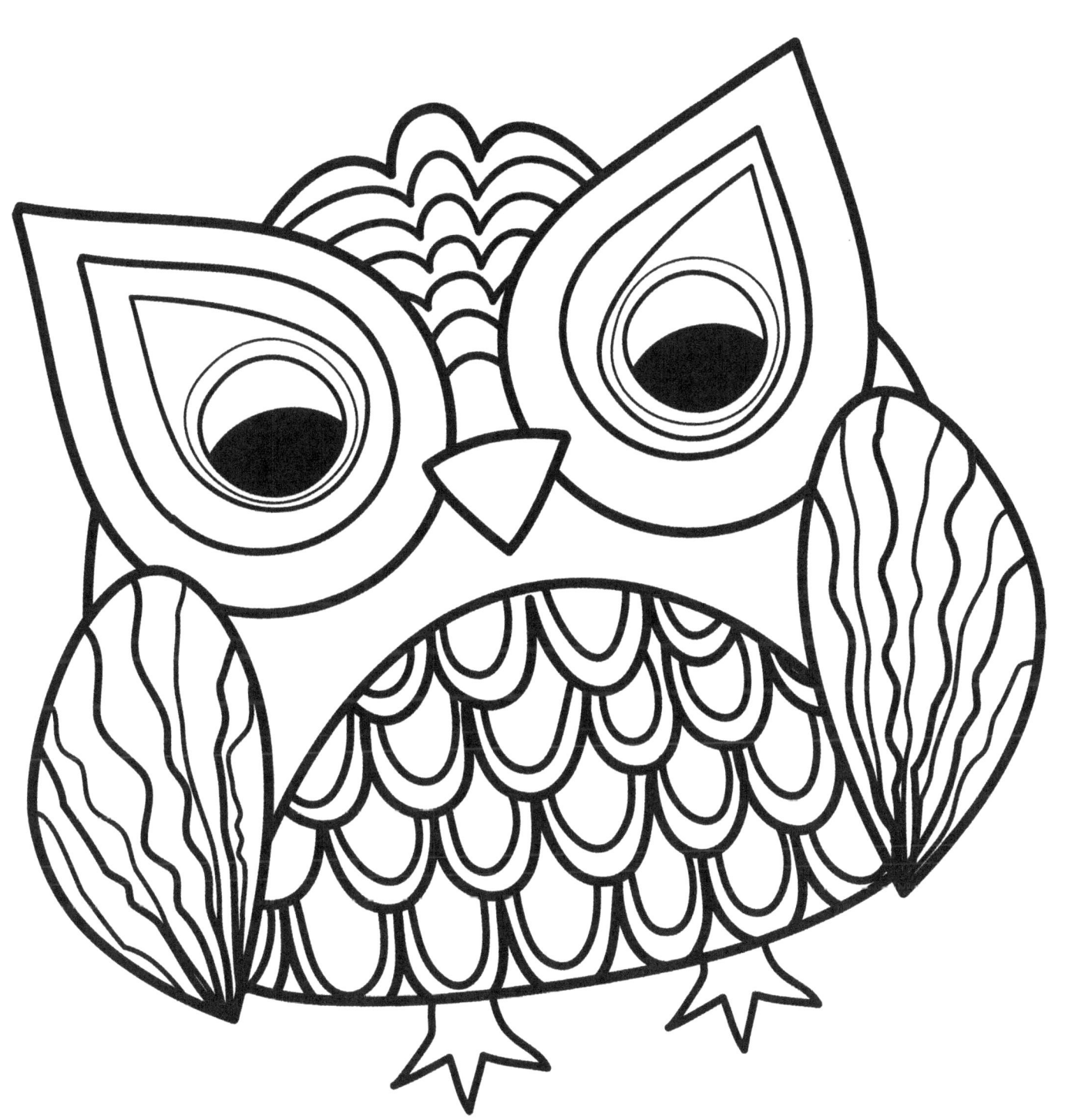

Large Print Adult Coloring Book: Owls and Other Birds

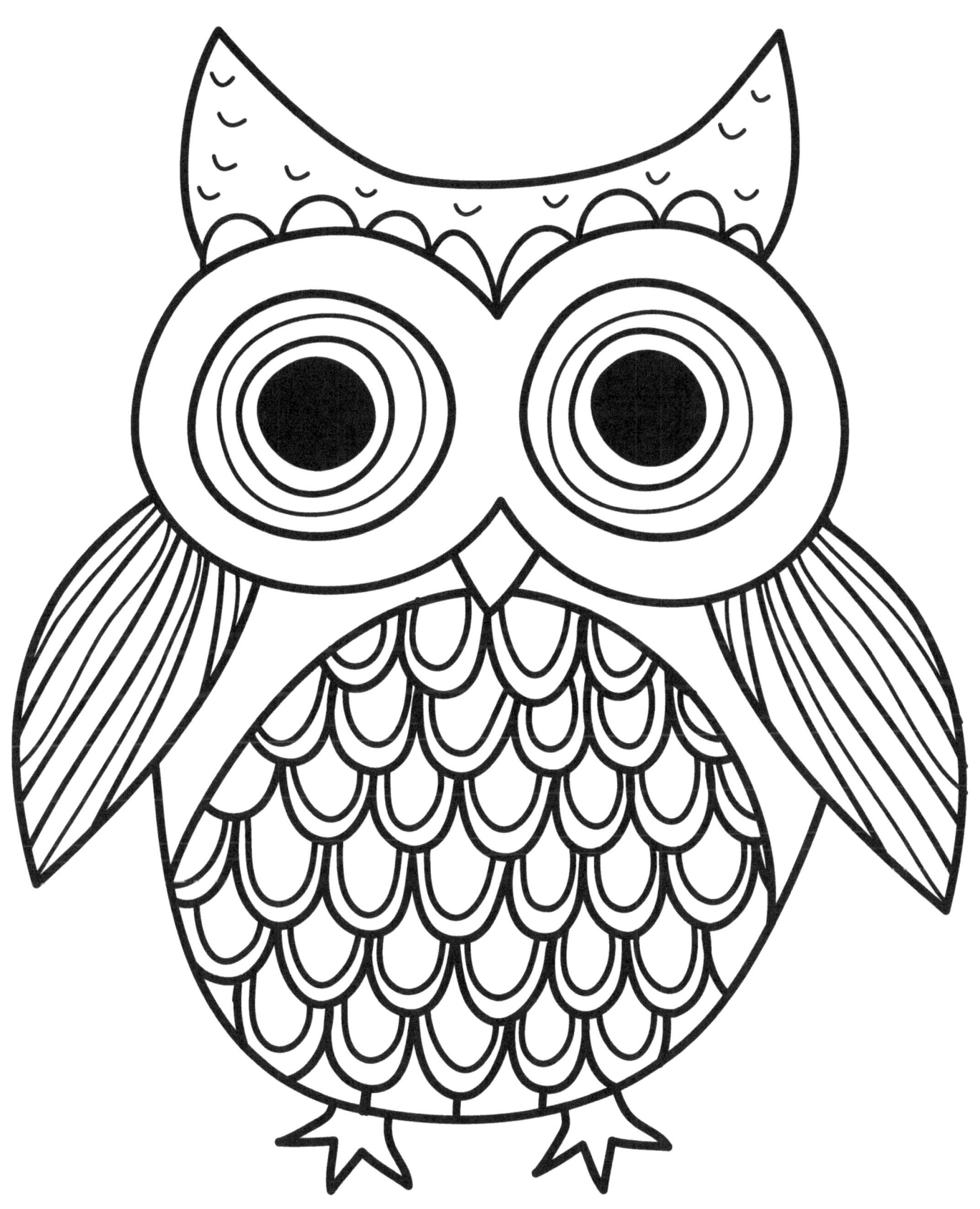

Large Print Adult Coloring Book: Owls and Other Birds

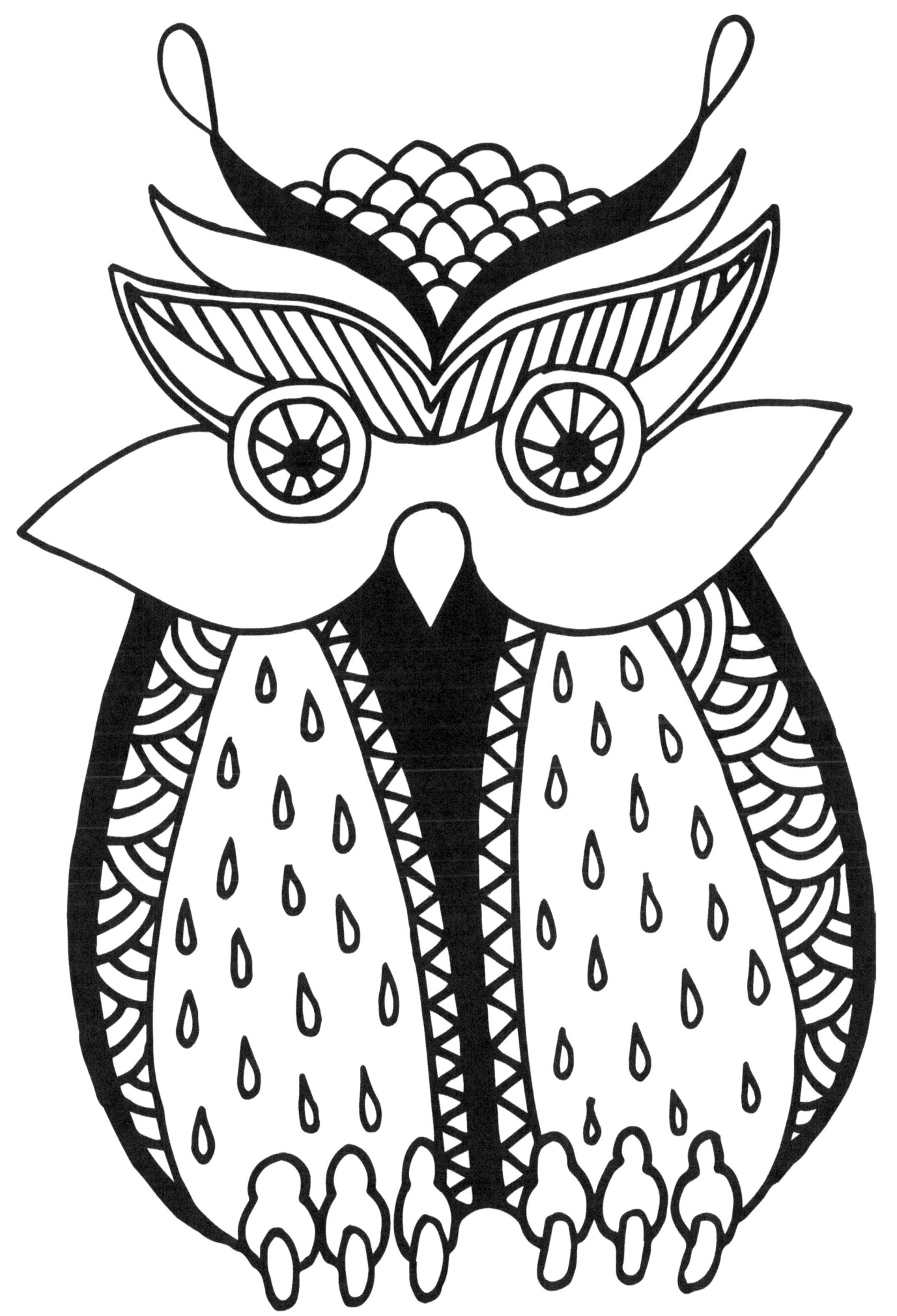

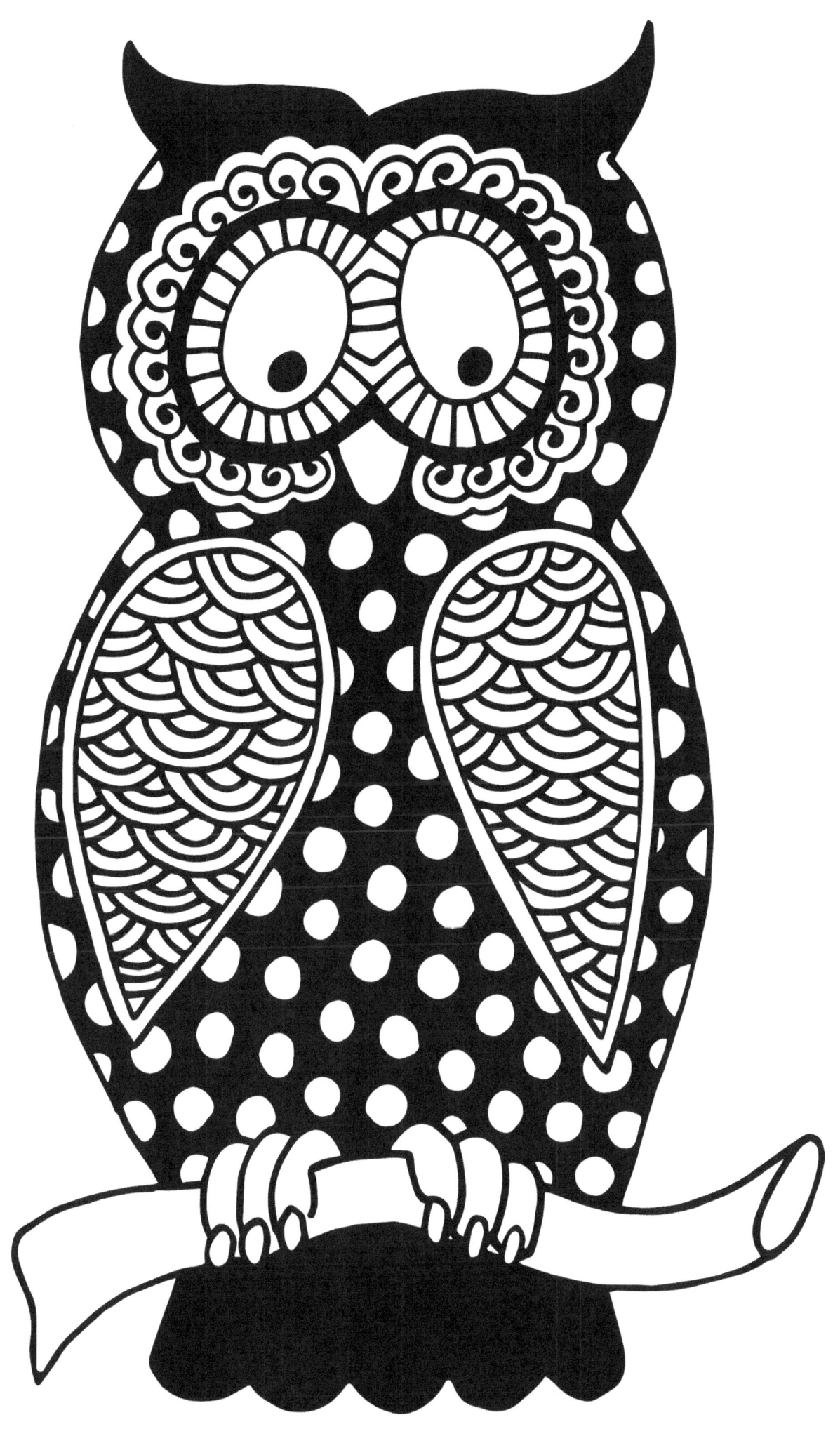

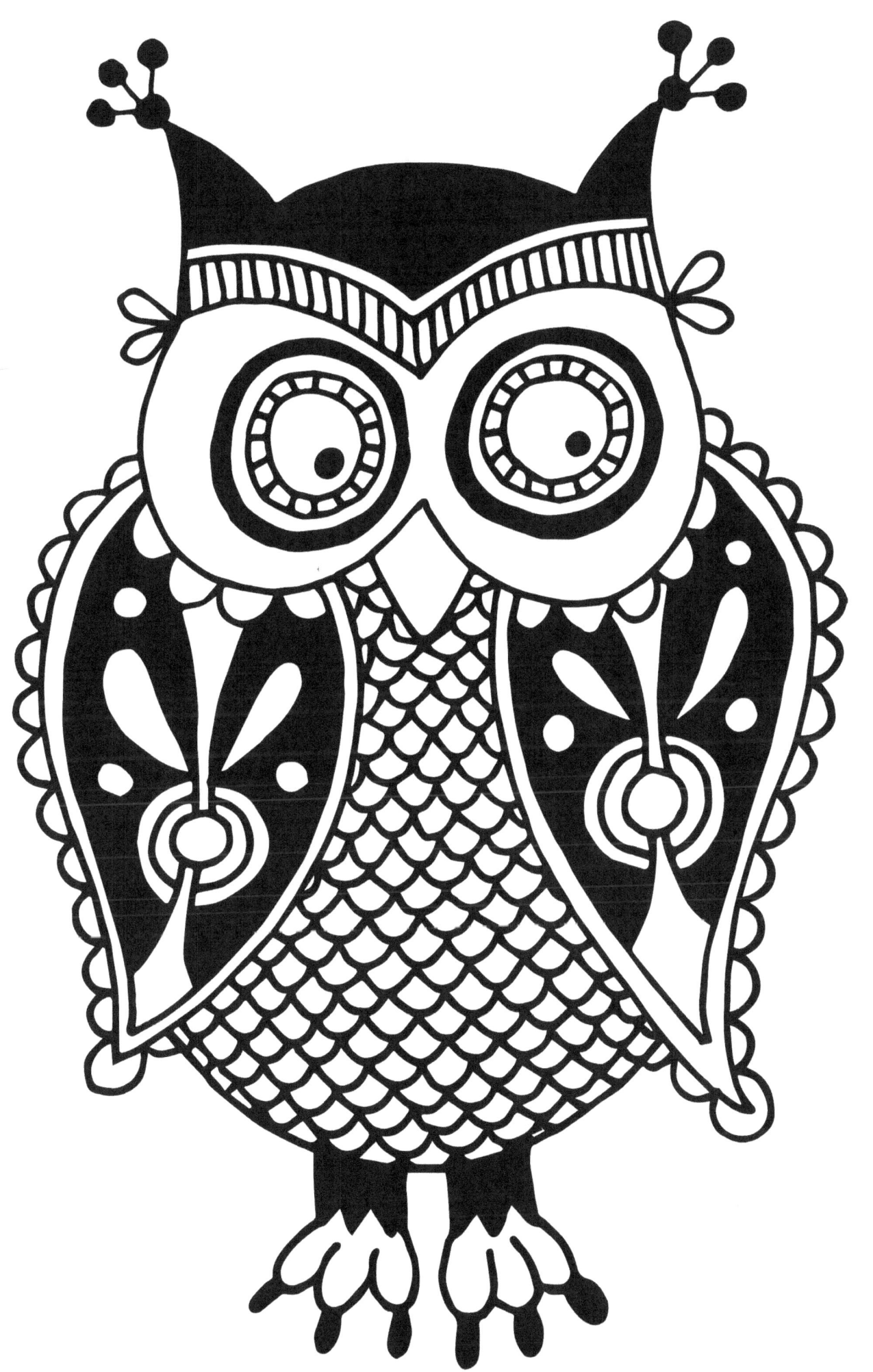

Large Print Adult Coloring Book: Owls and Other Birds

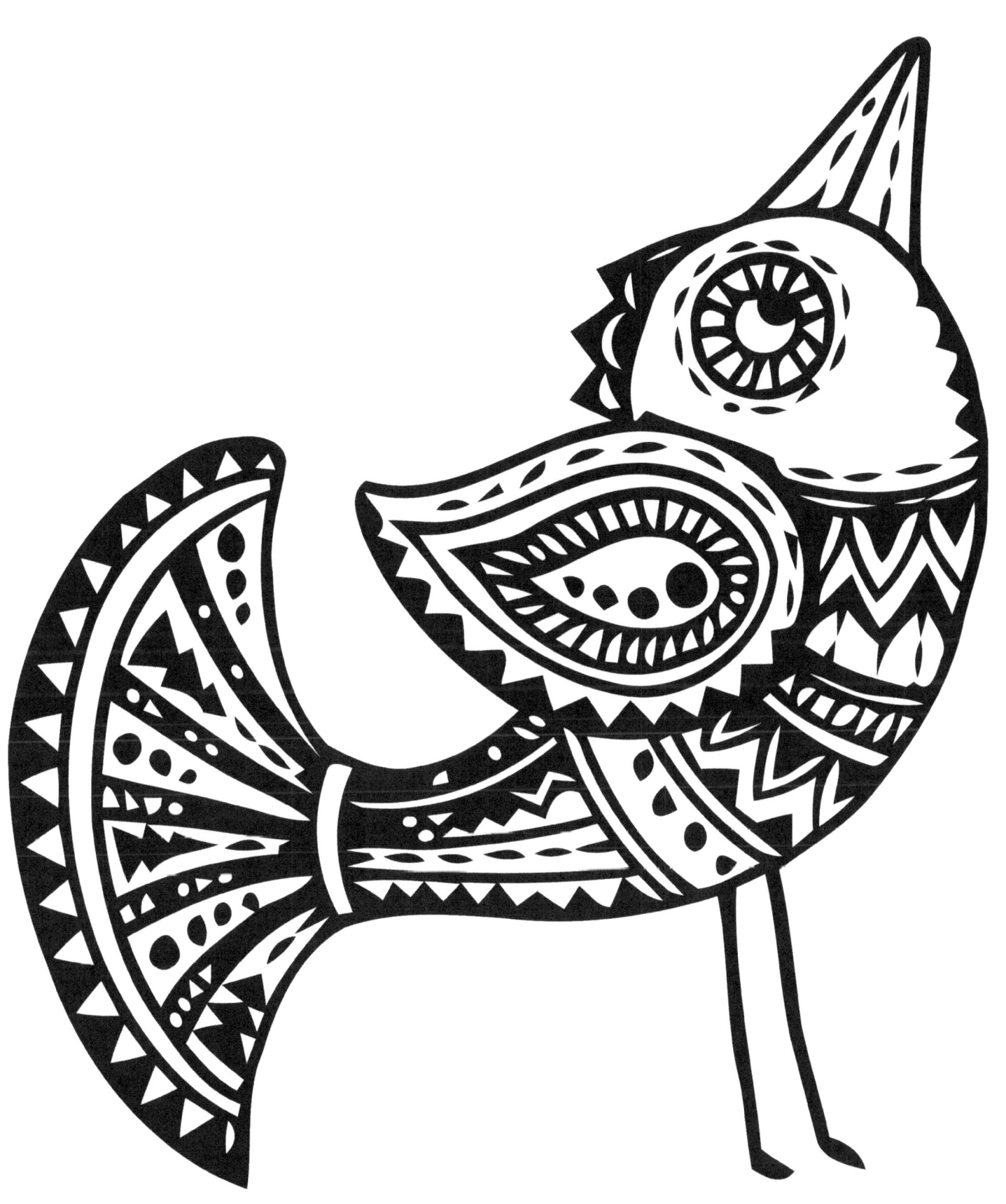

Large Print Adult Coloring Book: Owls and Other Birds

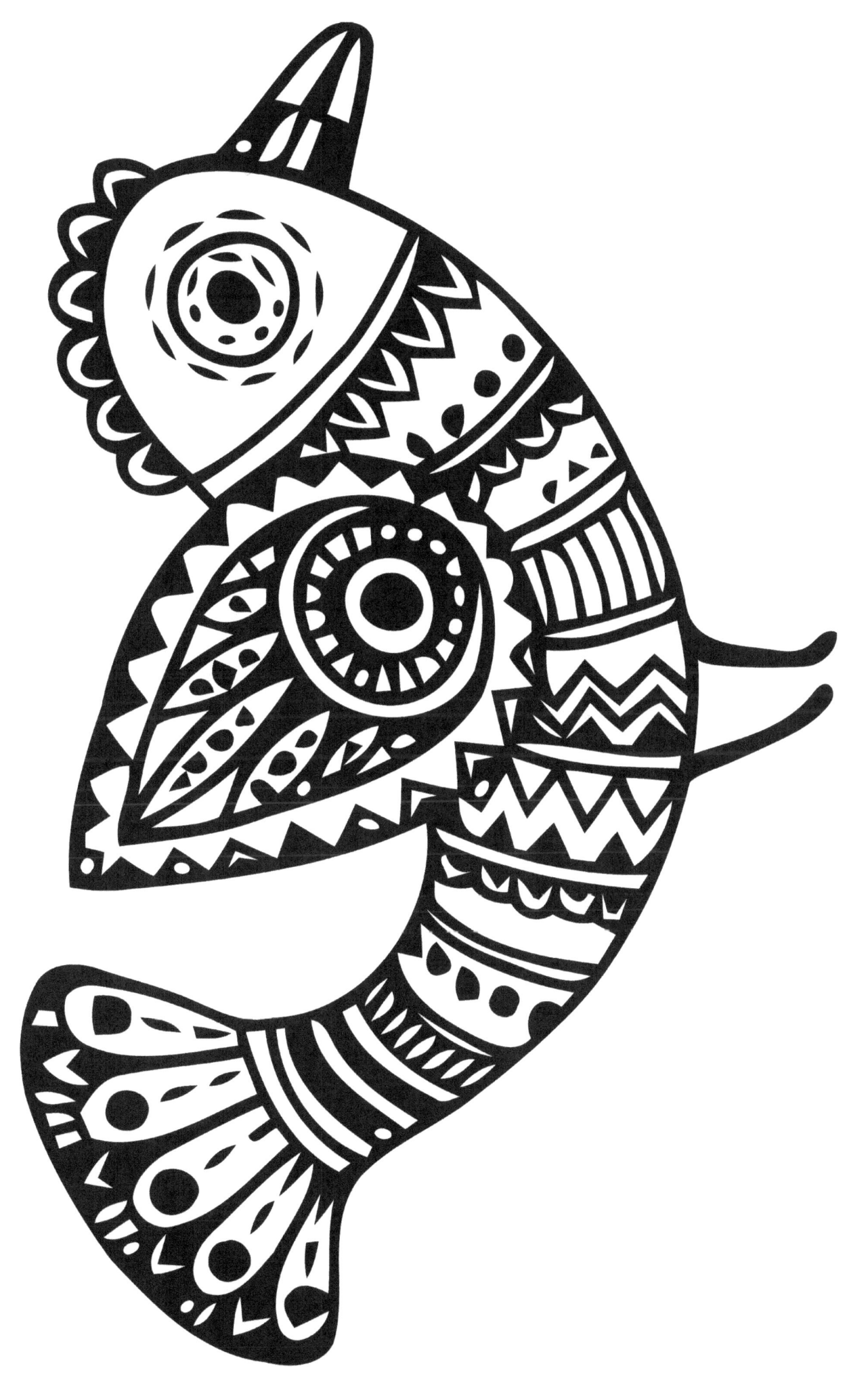

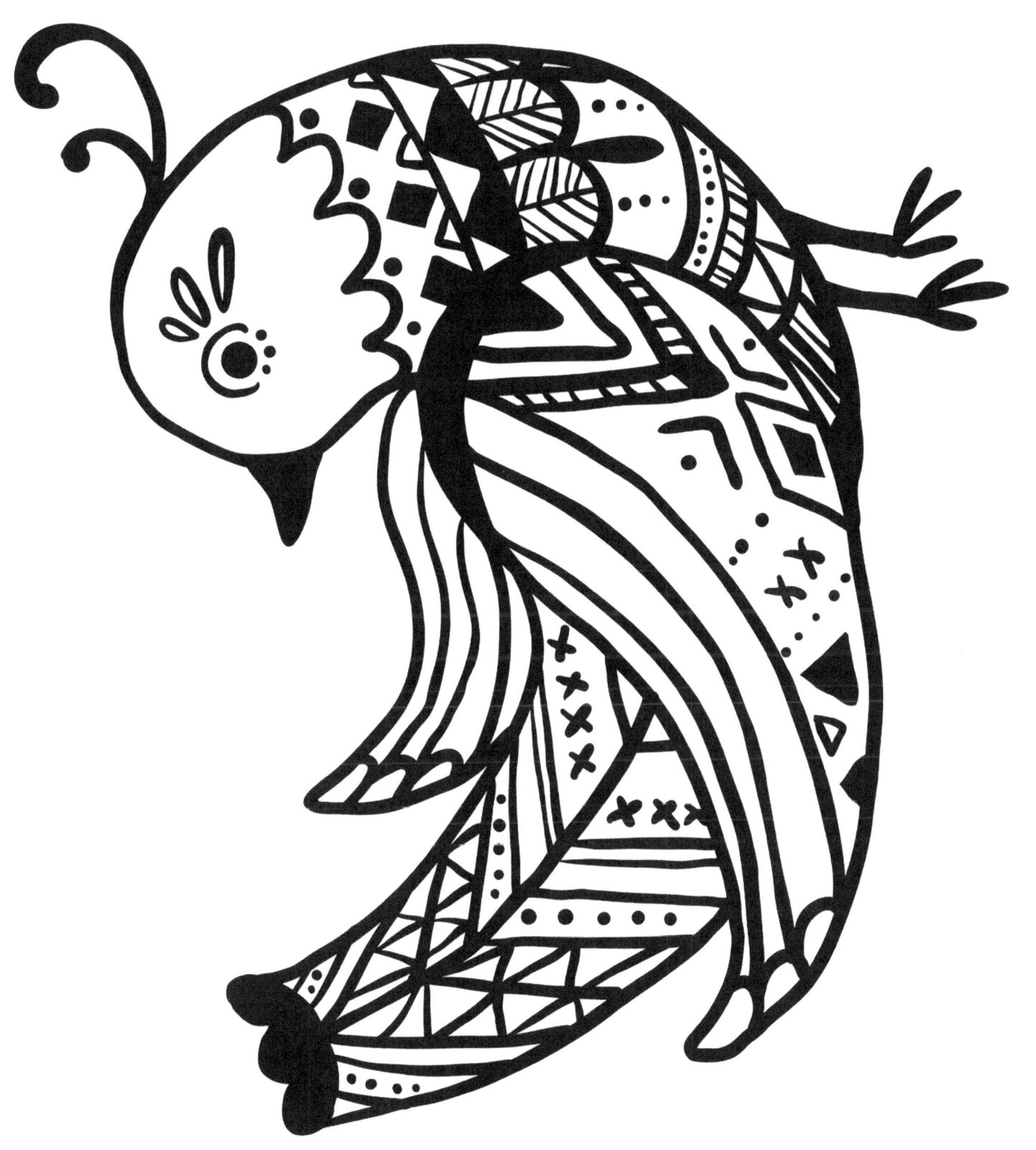

Large Print Adult Coloring Book: Owls and Other Birds

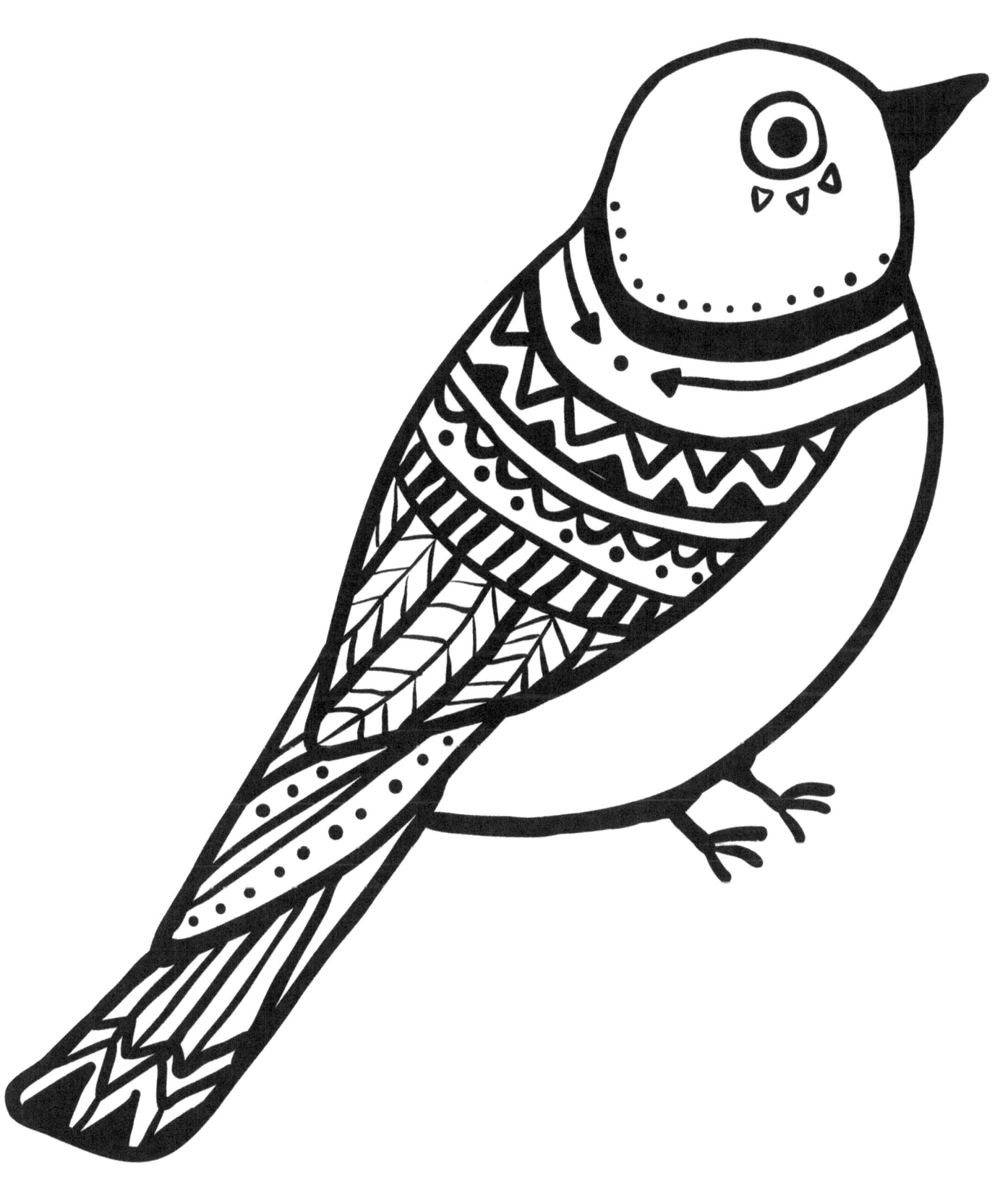

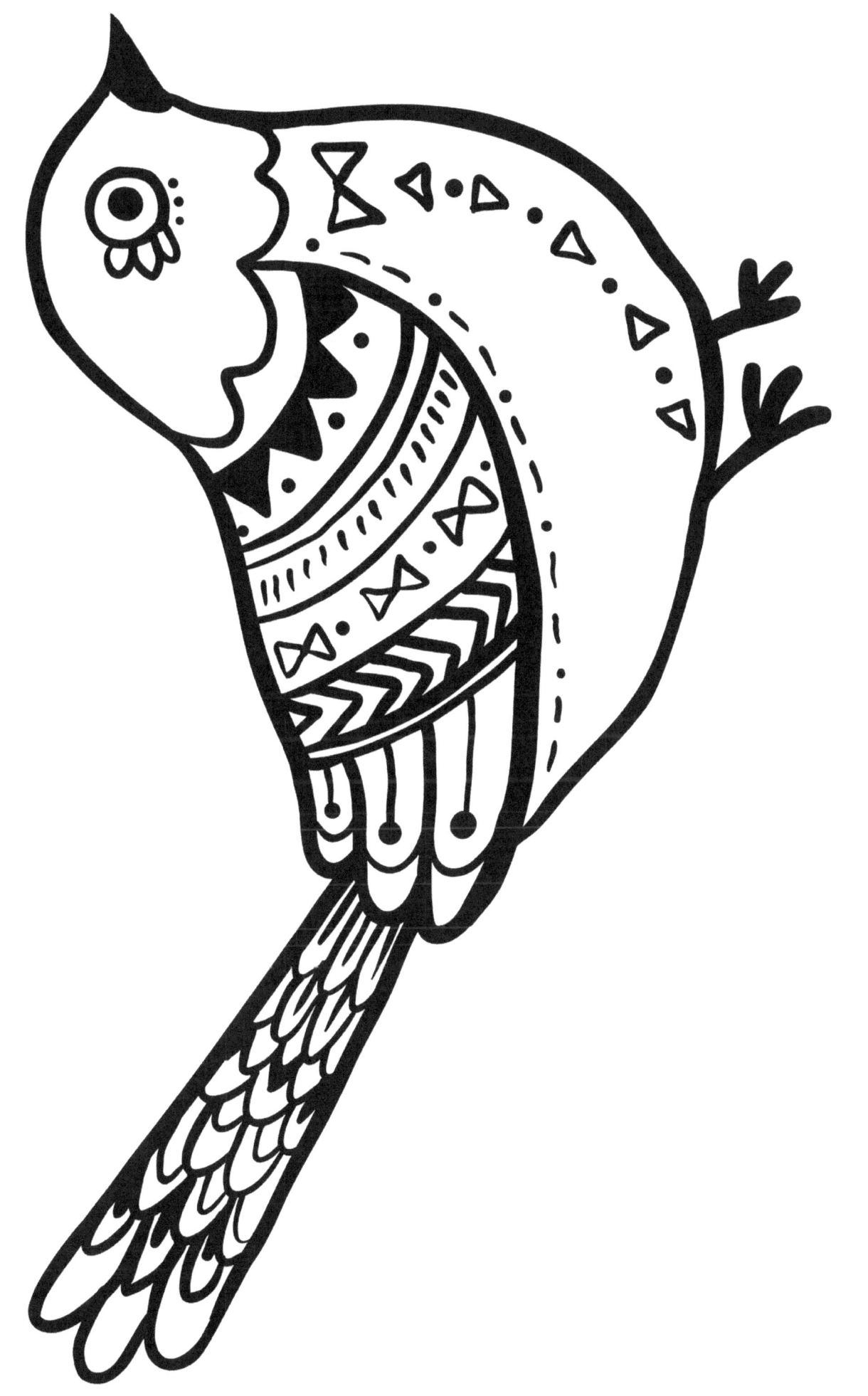

Large Print Adult Coloring Book: Owls and Other Birds

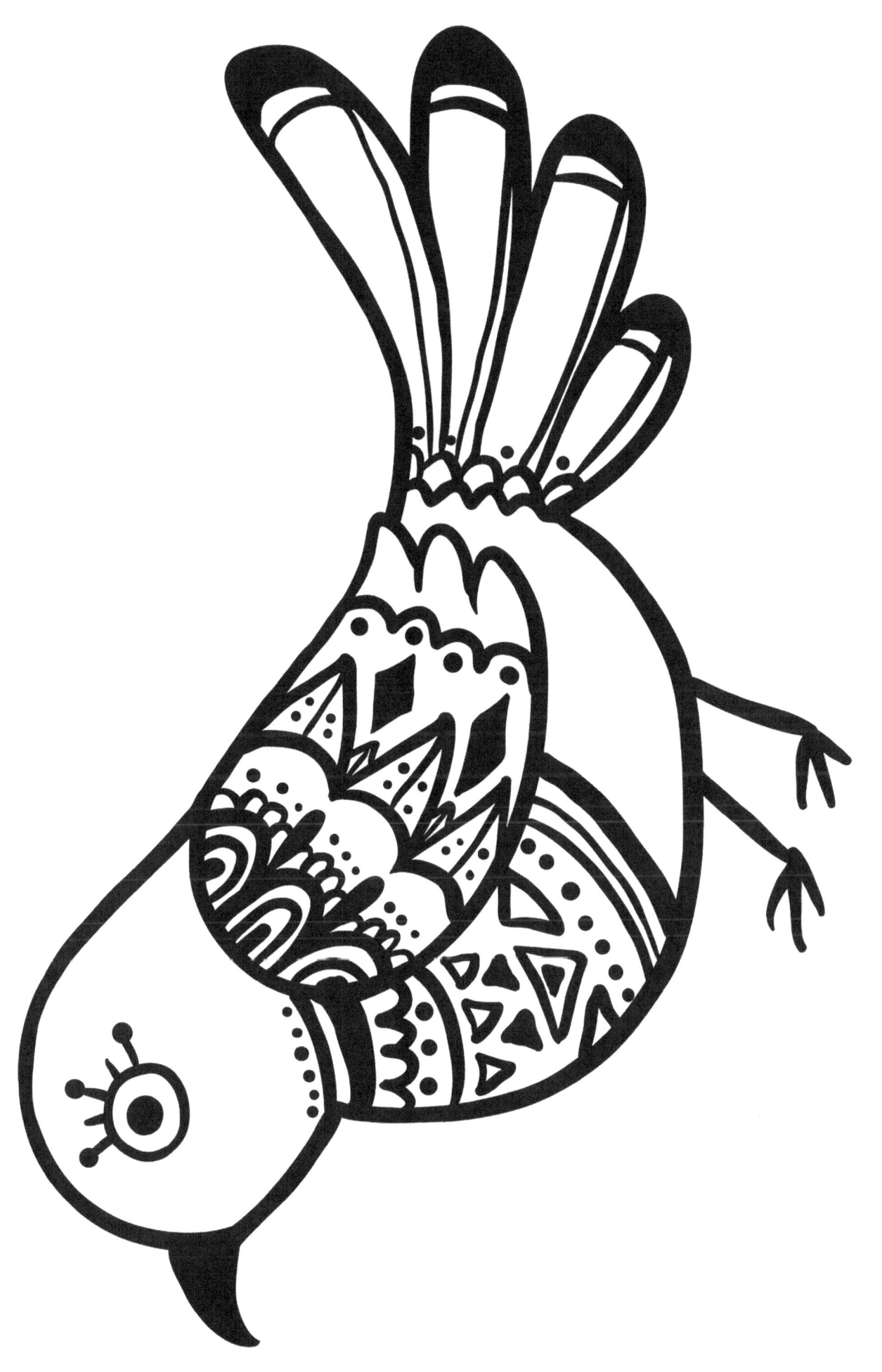

Large Print Adult Coloring Book: Owls and Other Birds

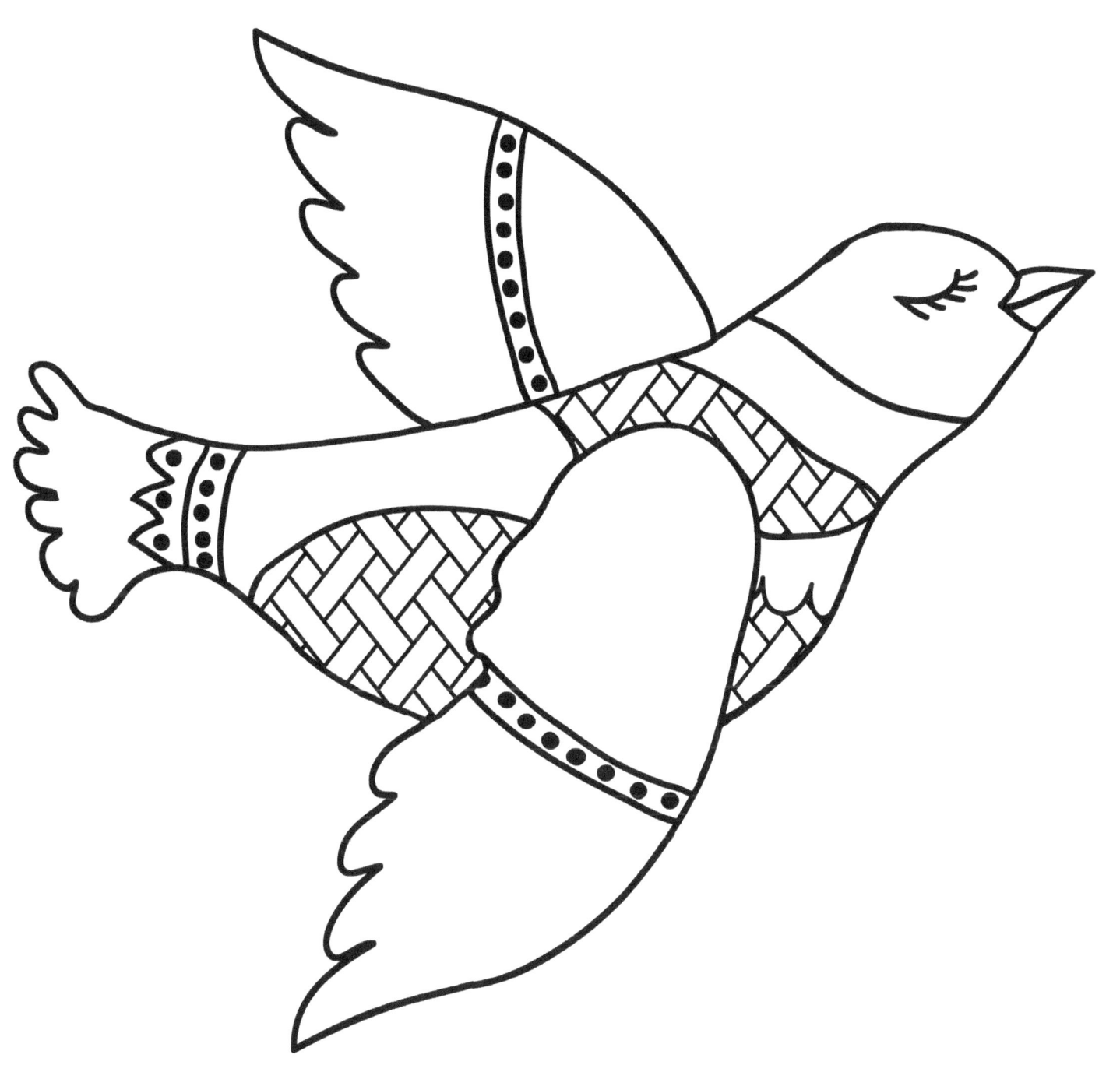

Large Print Adult Coloring Book: Owls and Other Birds

© Synchronista LLC

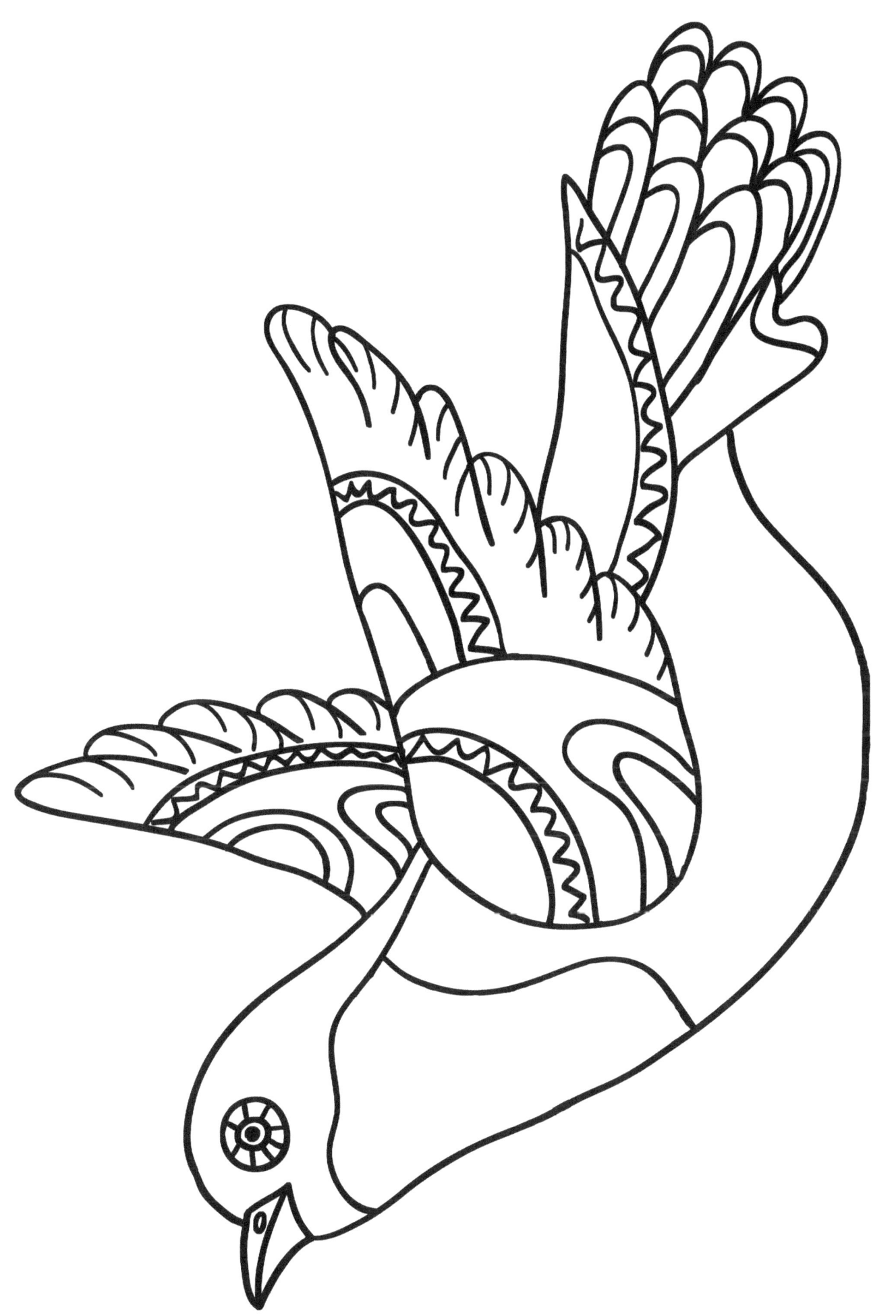

Large Print Adult Coloring Book: Owls and Other Birds

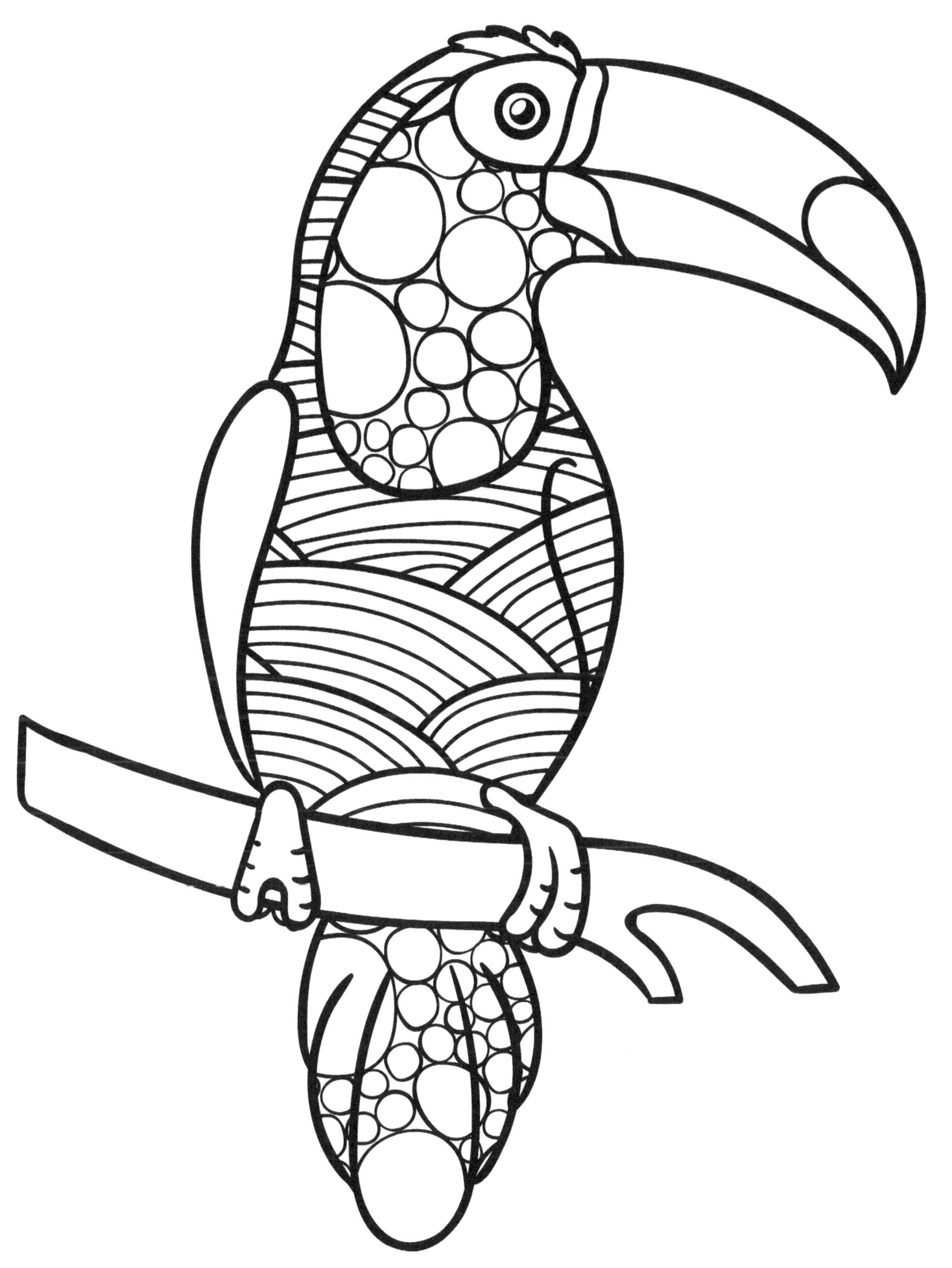

Large Print Adult Coloring Book: Owls and Other Birds

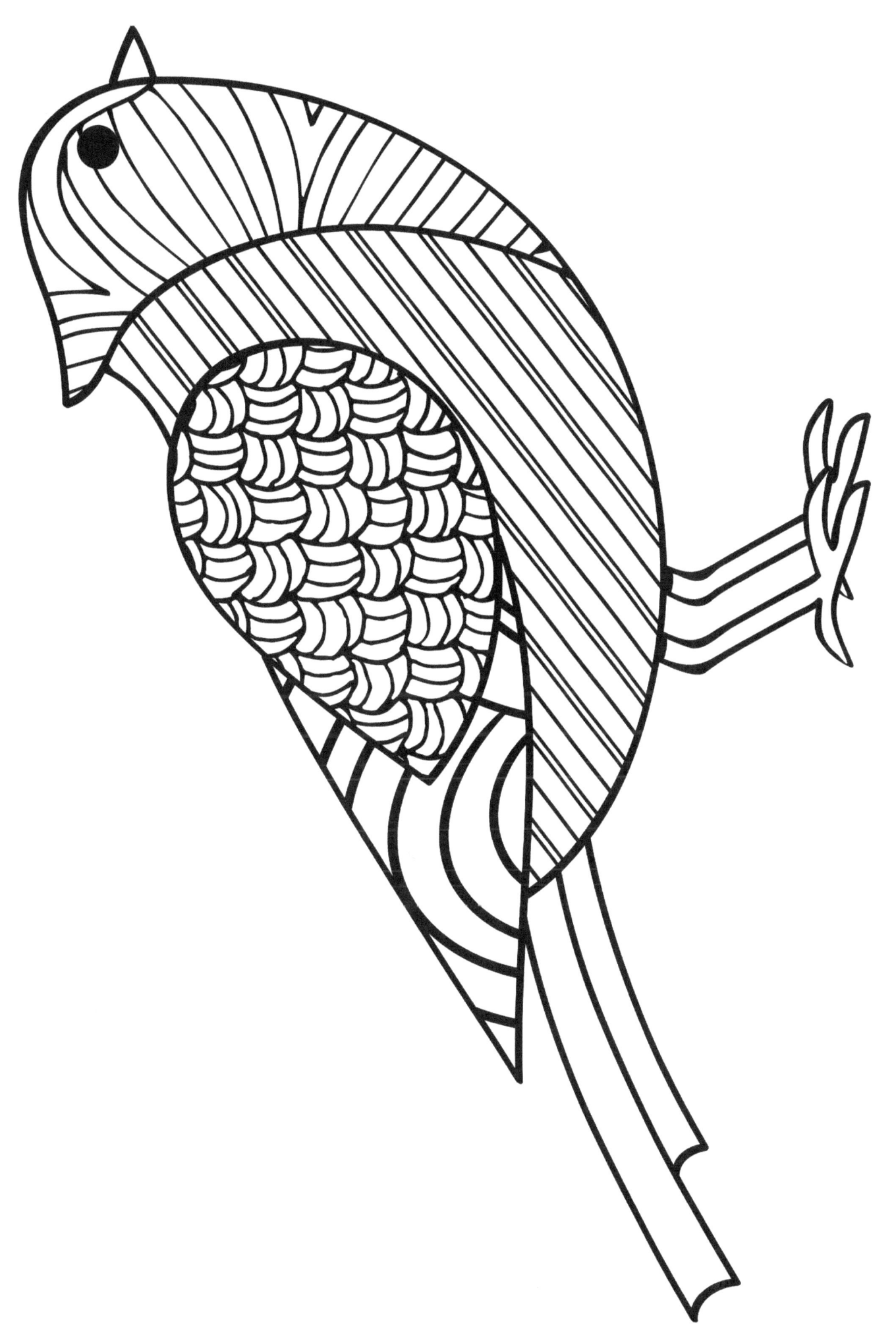

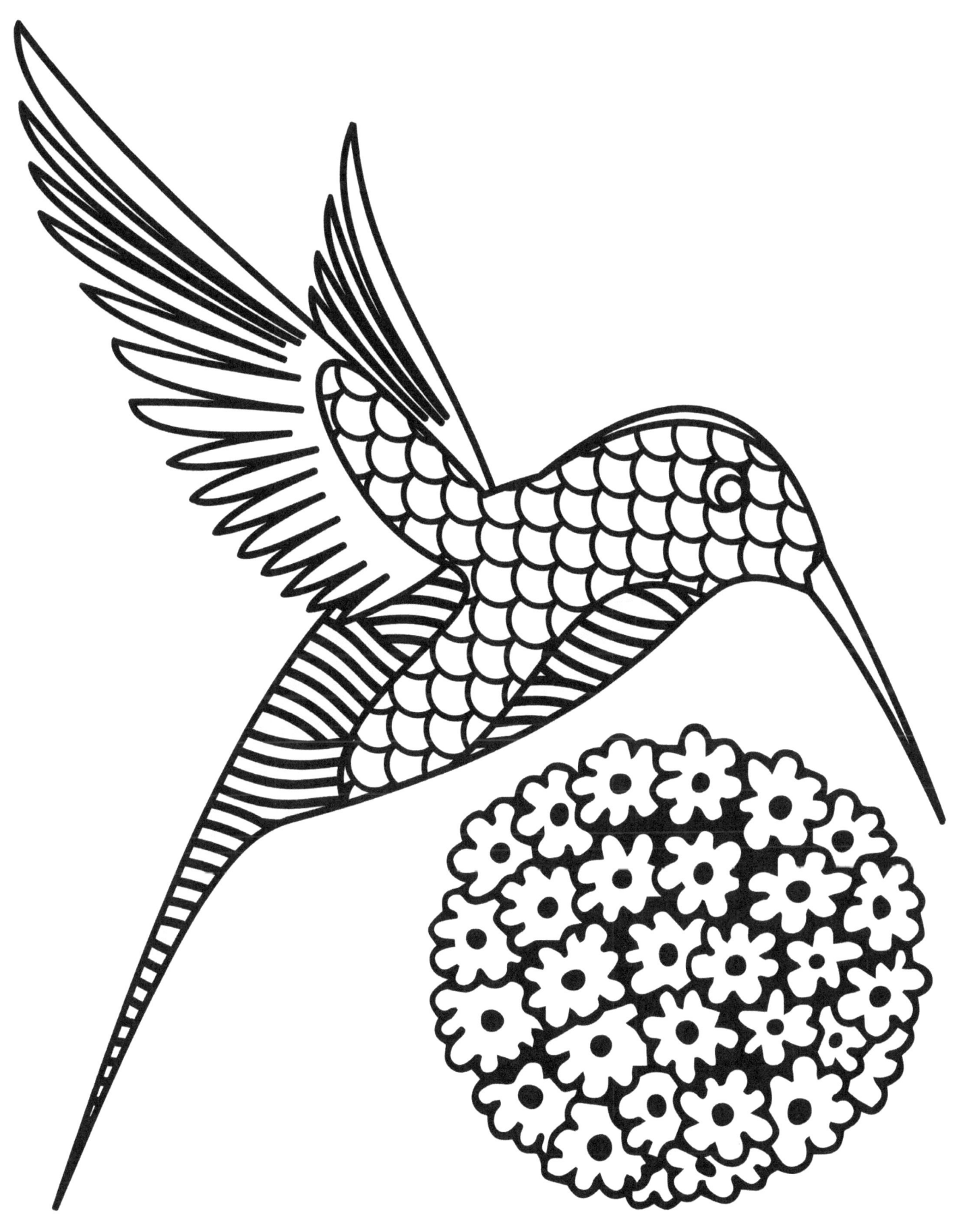

Large Print Adult Coloring Book: Owls and Other Birds

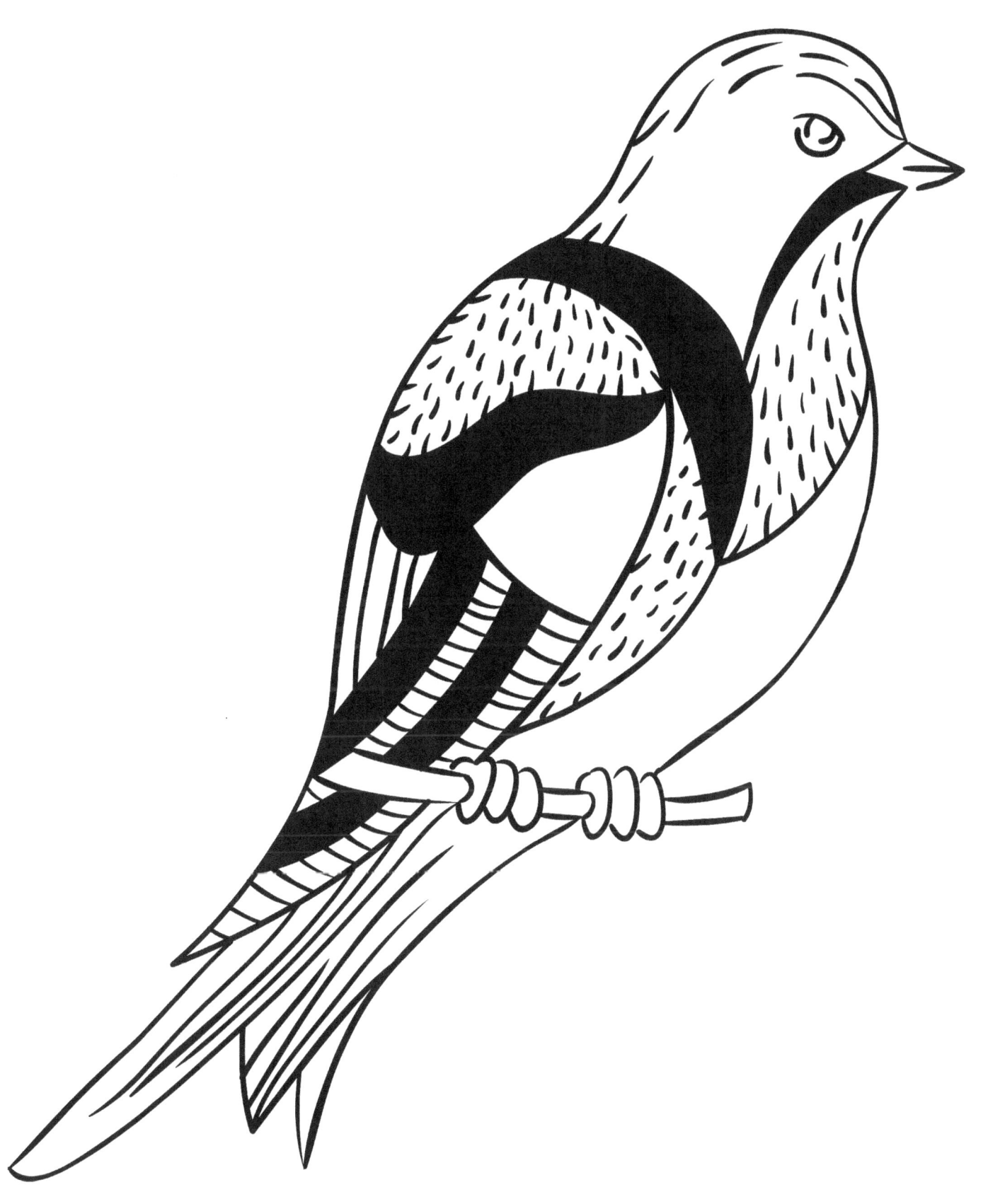

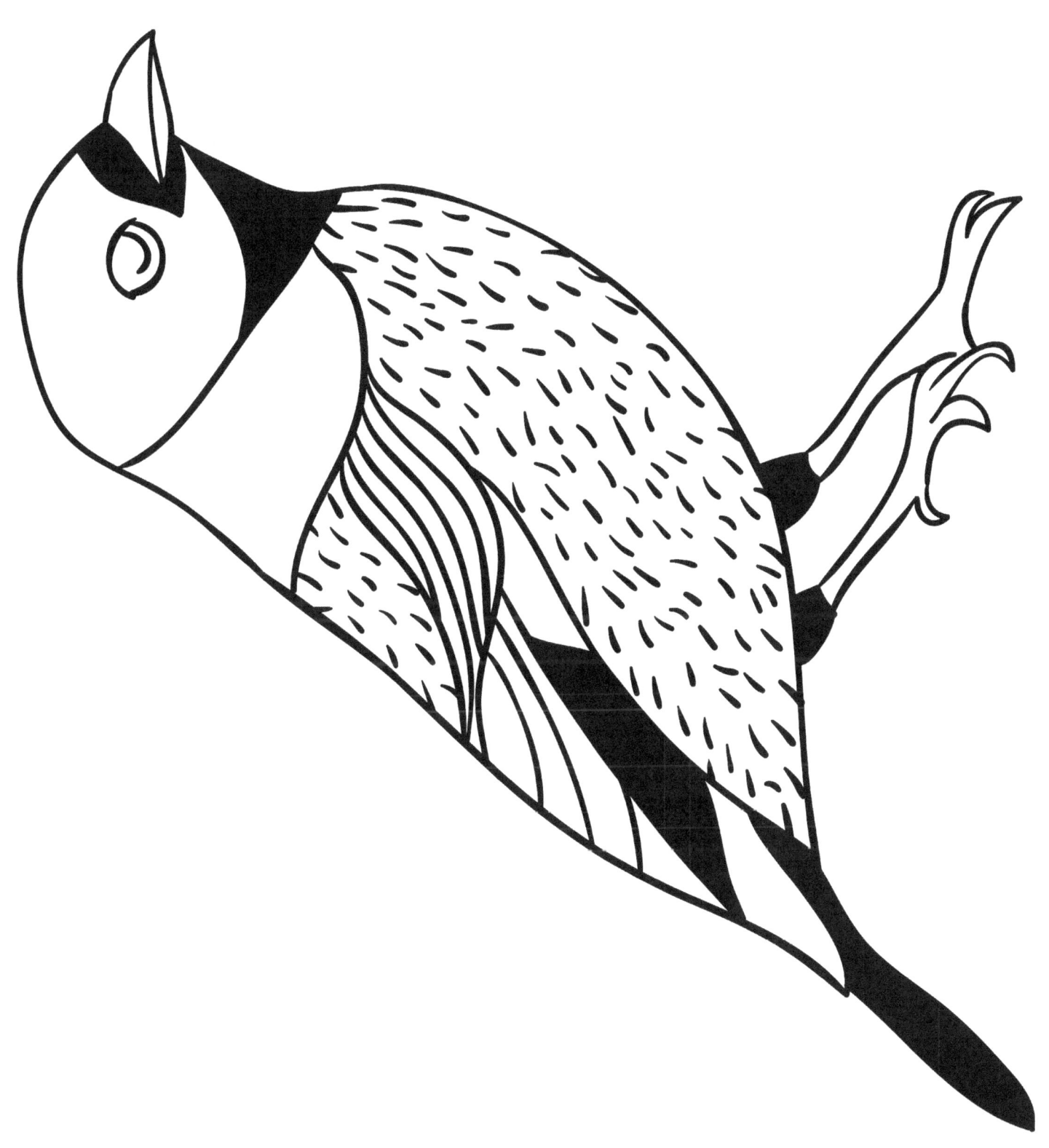

Large Print Adult Coloring Book: Owls and Other Birds

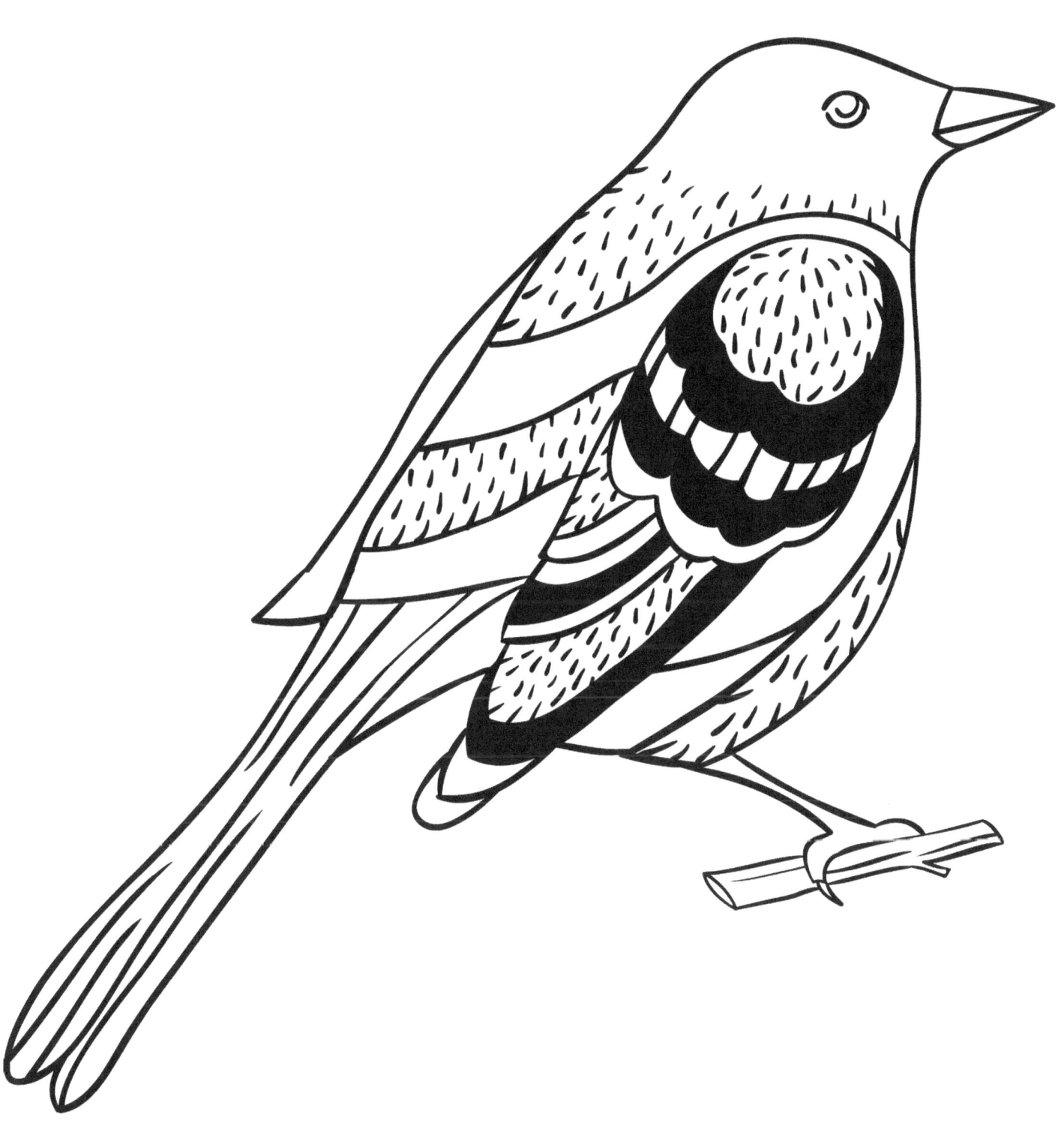

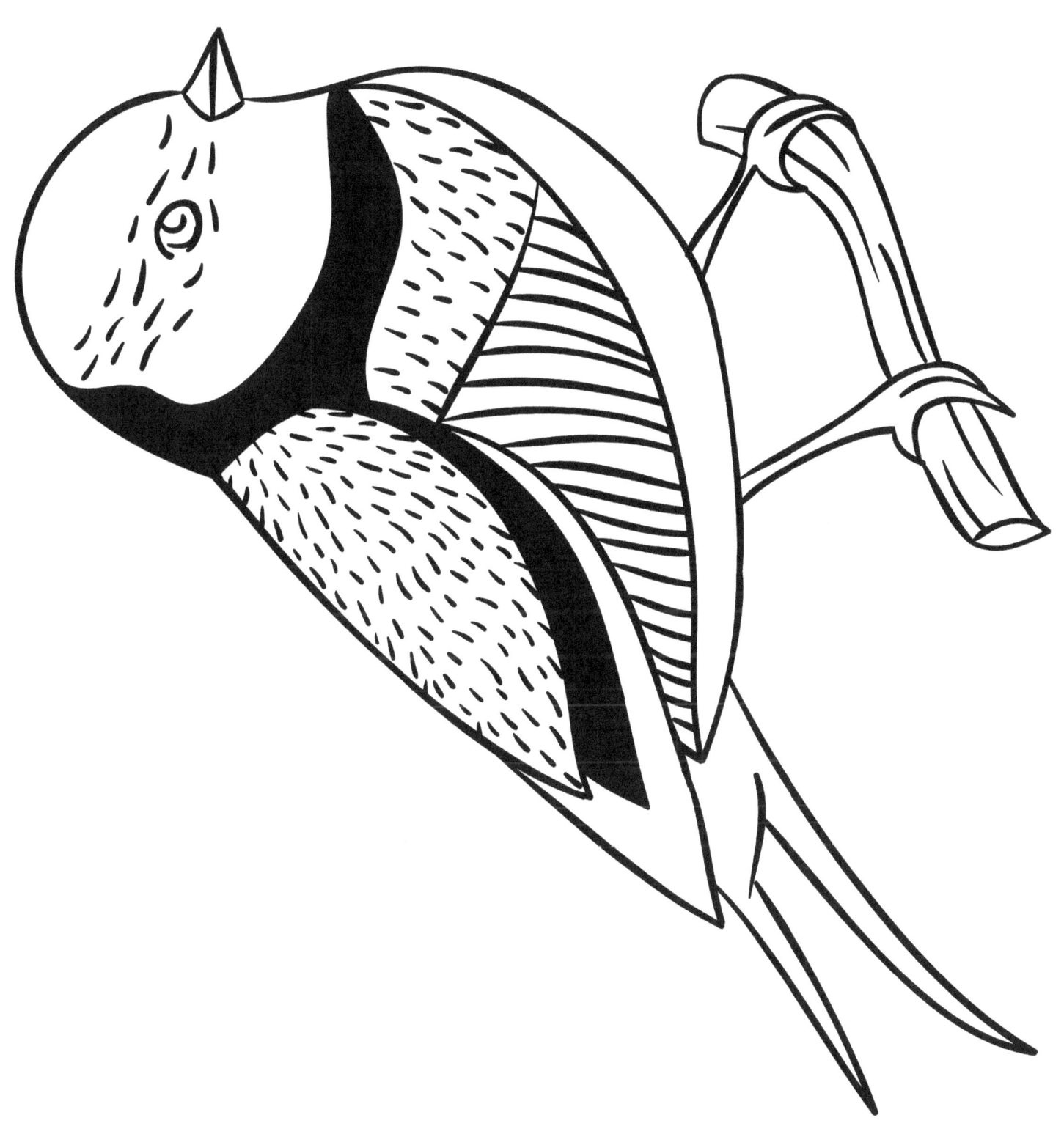

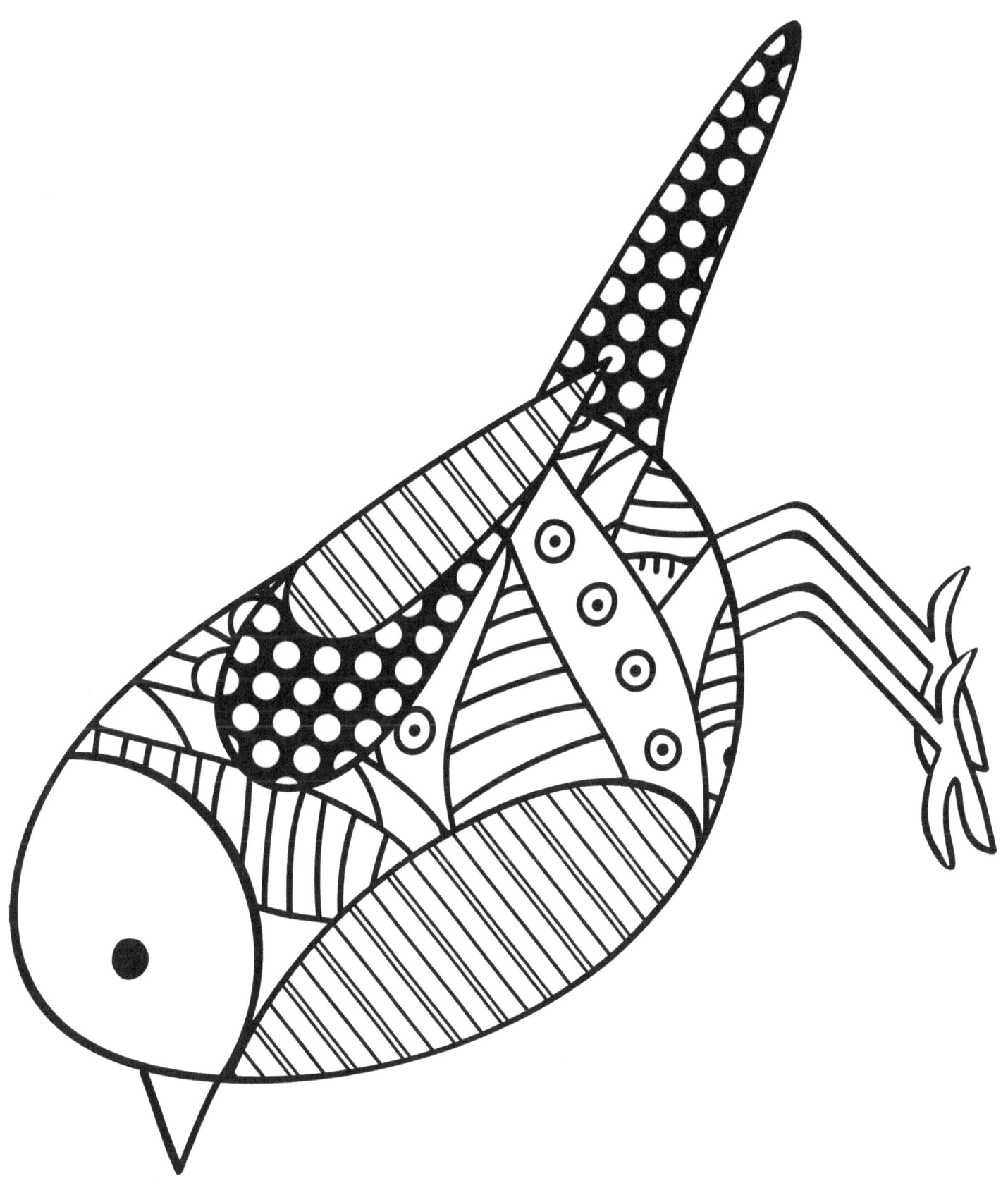

Large Print Adult Coloring Book: Owls and Other Birds

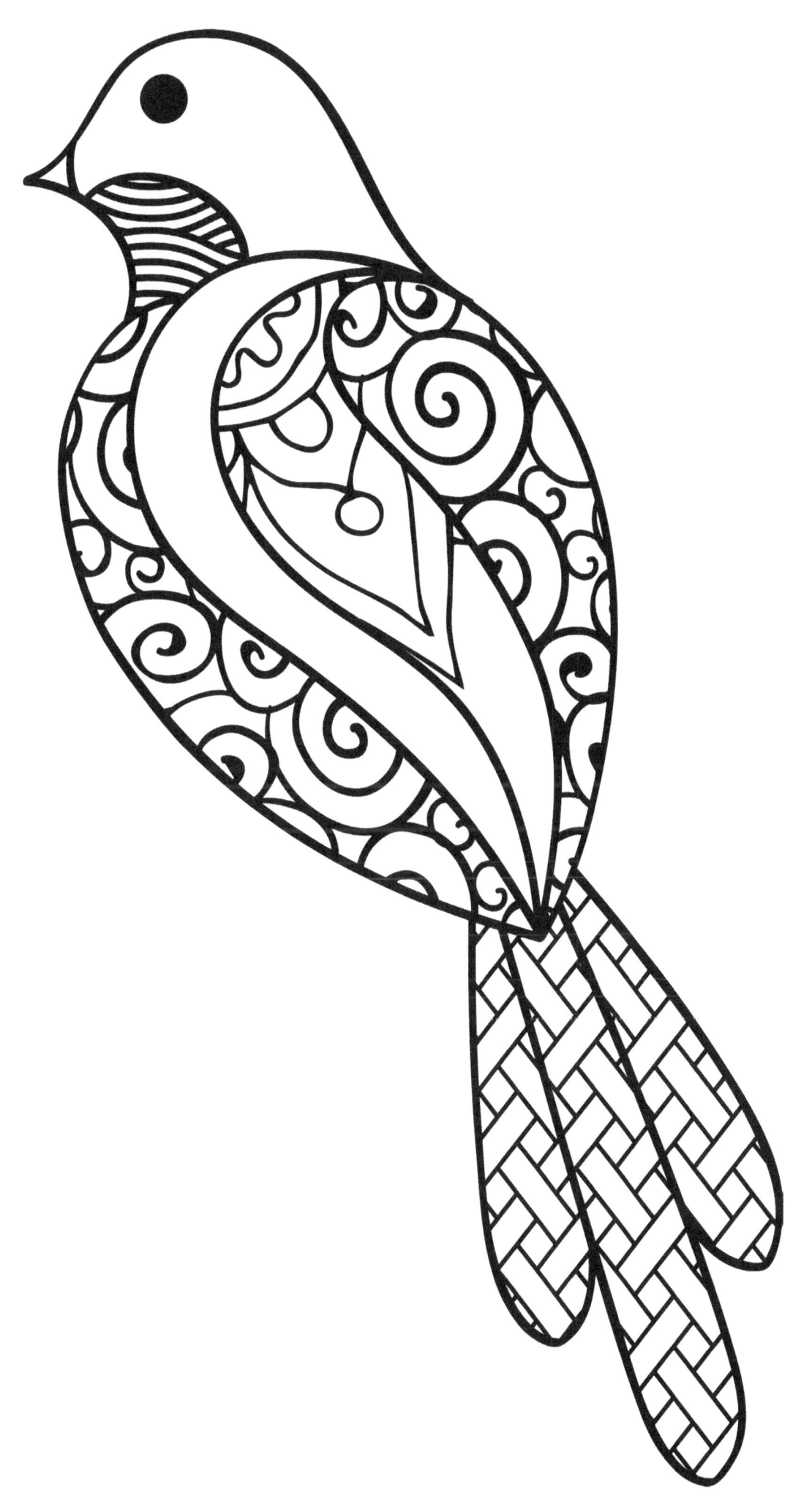

Large Print Adult Coloring Book: Owls and Other Birds

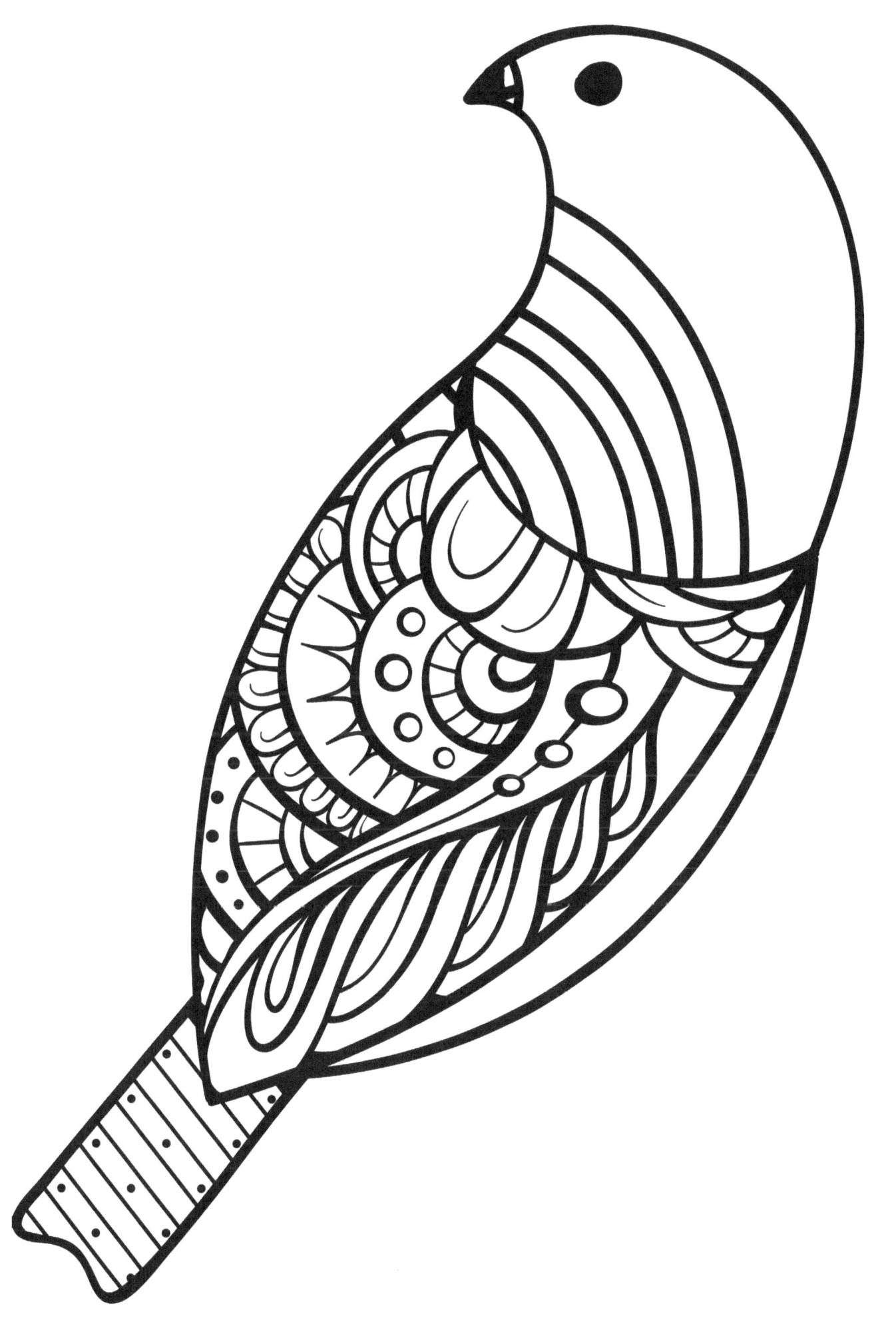

Large Print Adult Coloring Book: Owls and Other Birds

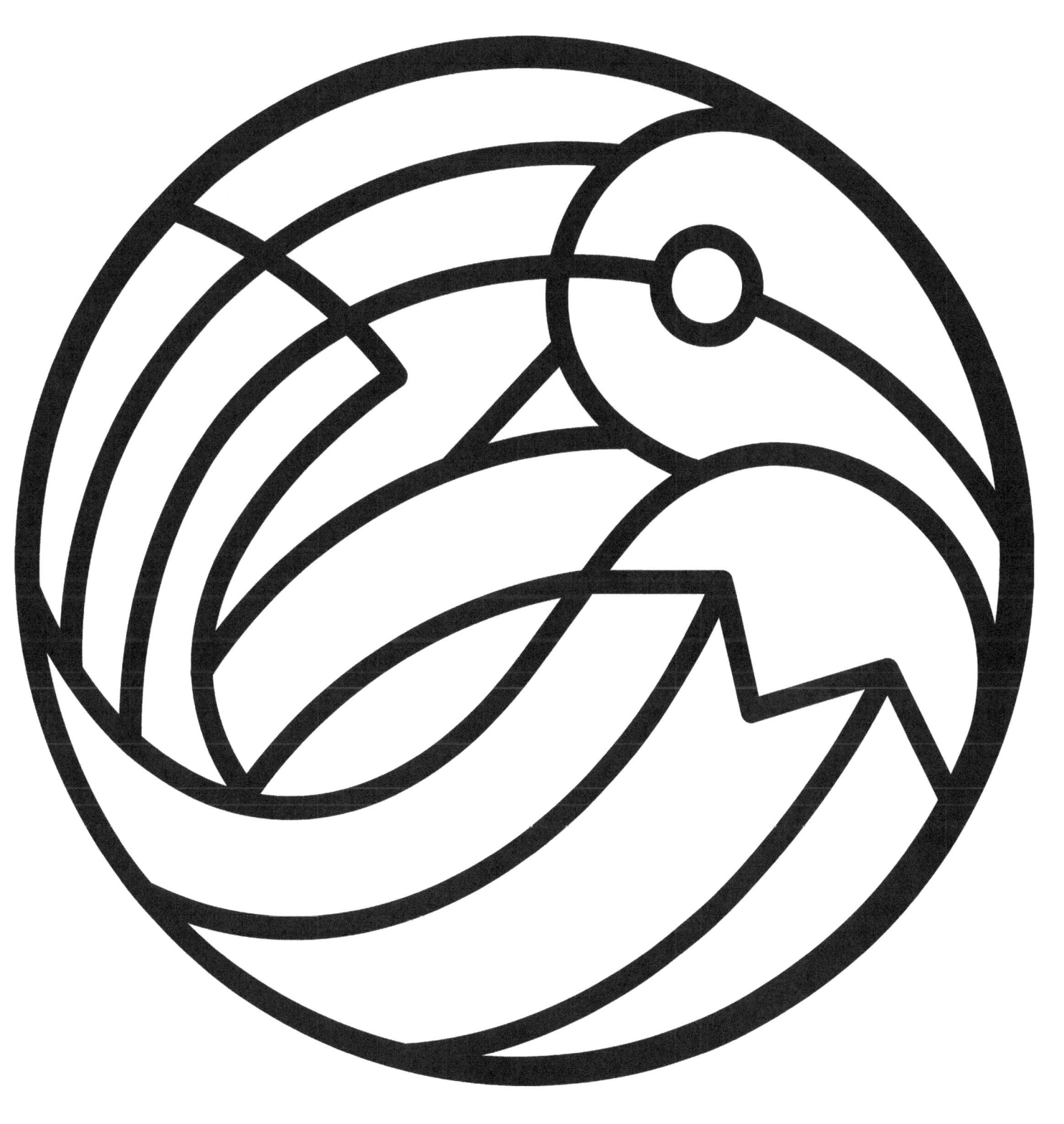

Large Print Adult Coloring Book: Owls and Other Birds

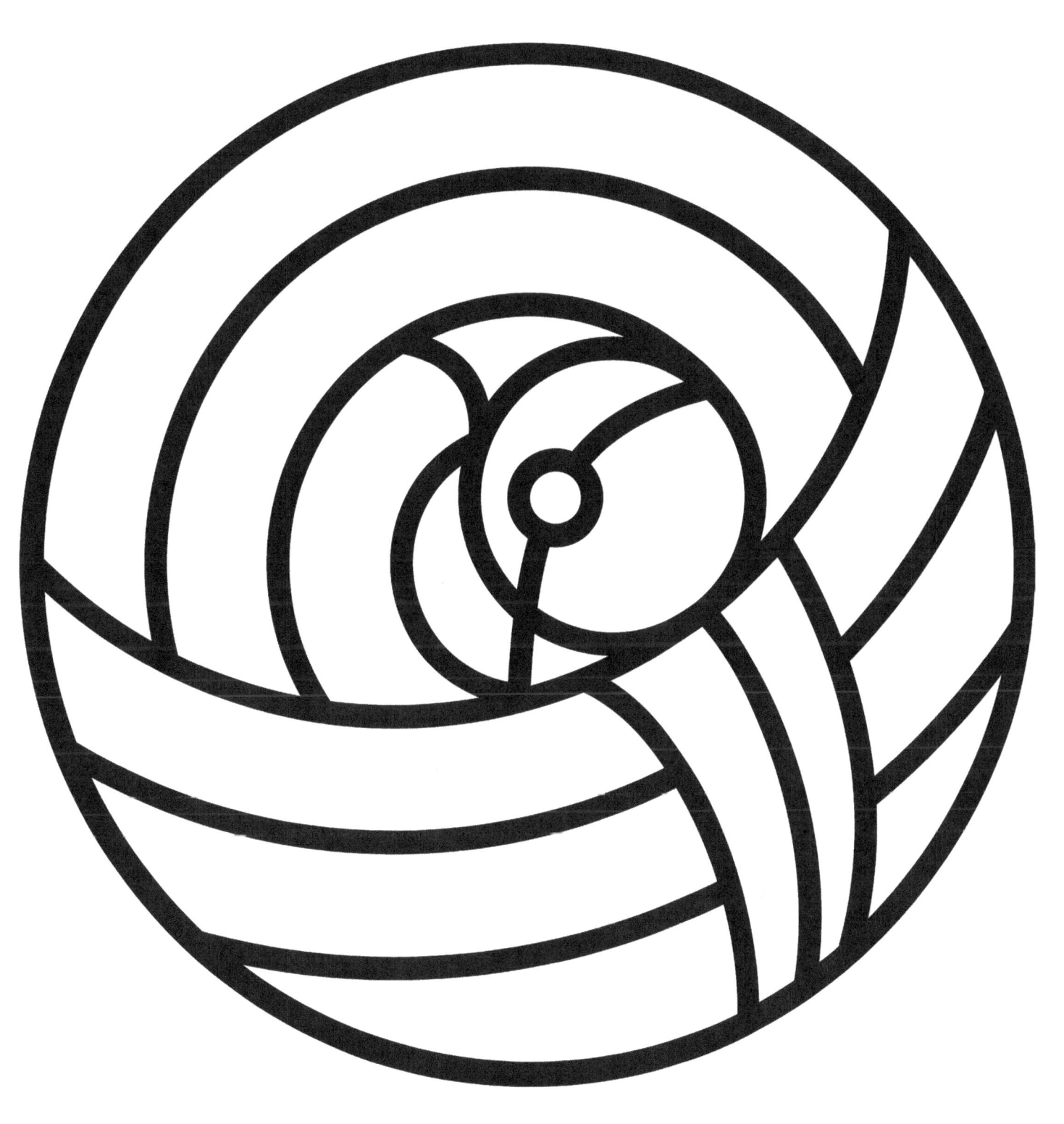

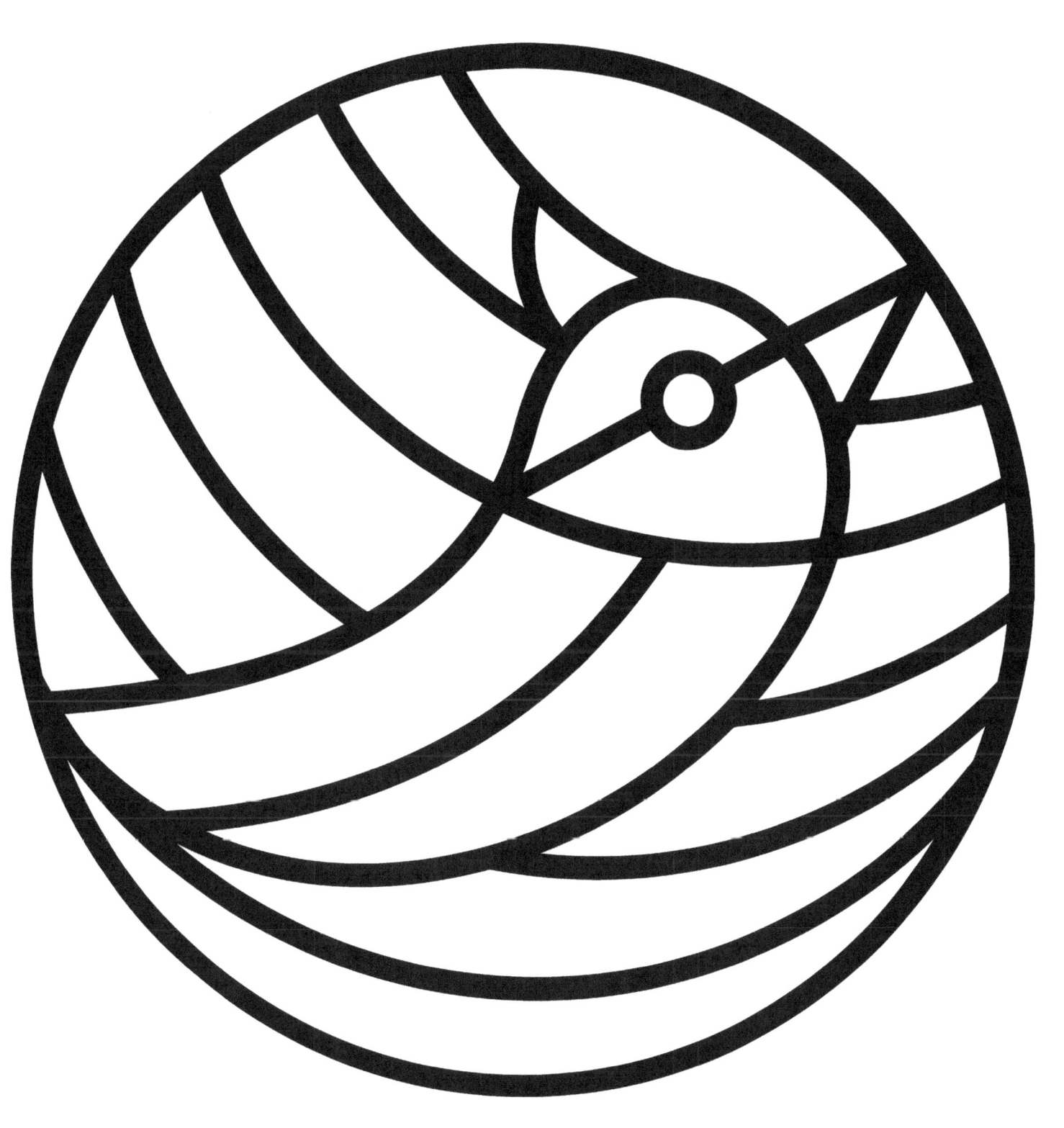

Large Print Adult Coloring Book: Owls and Other Birds

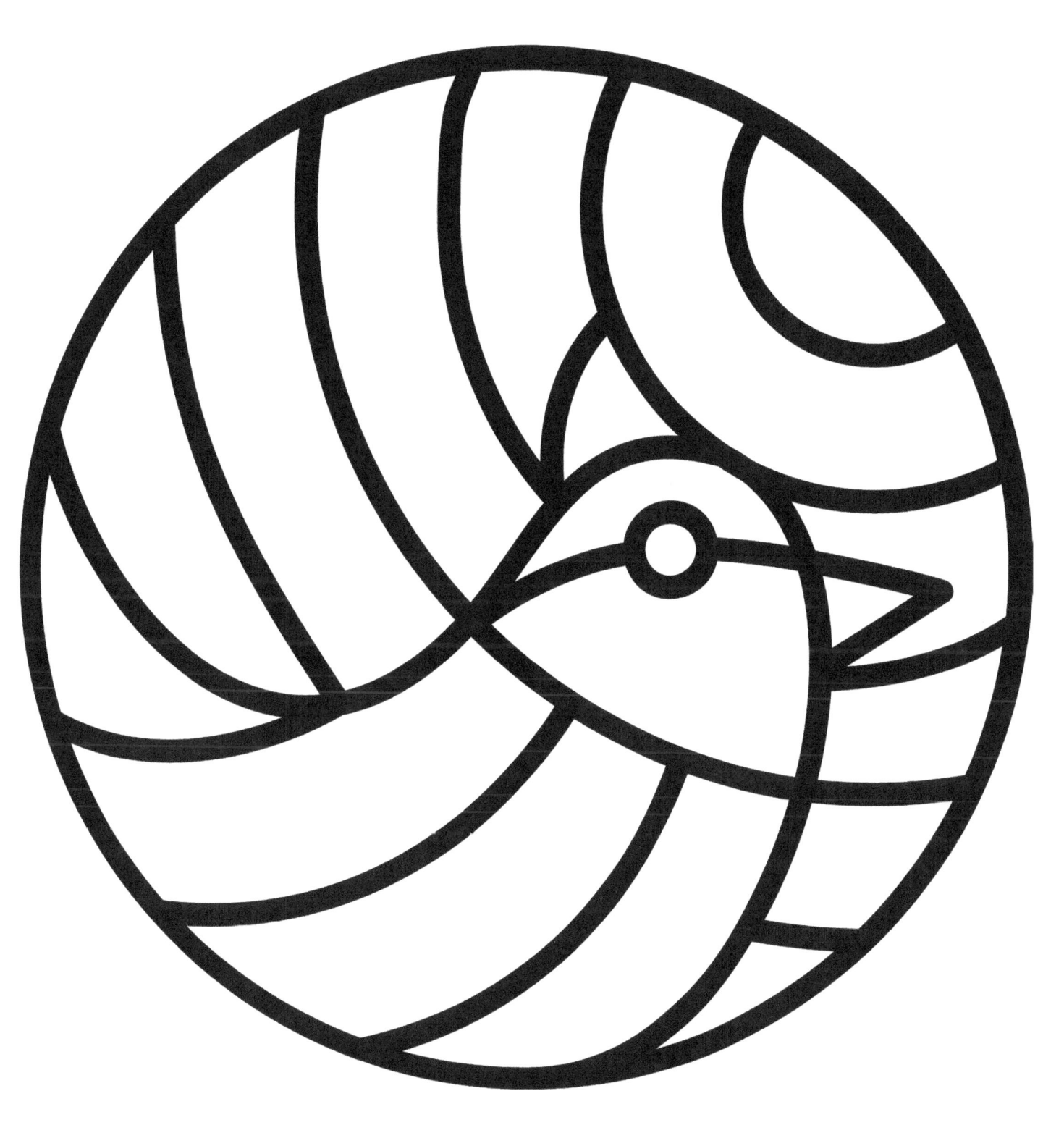

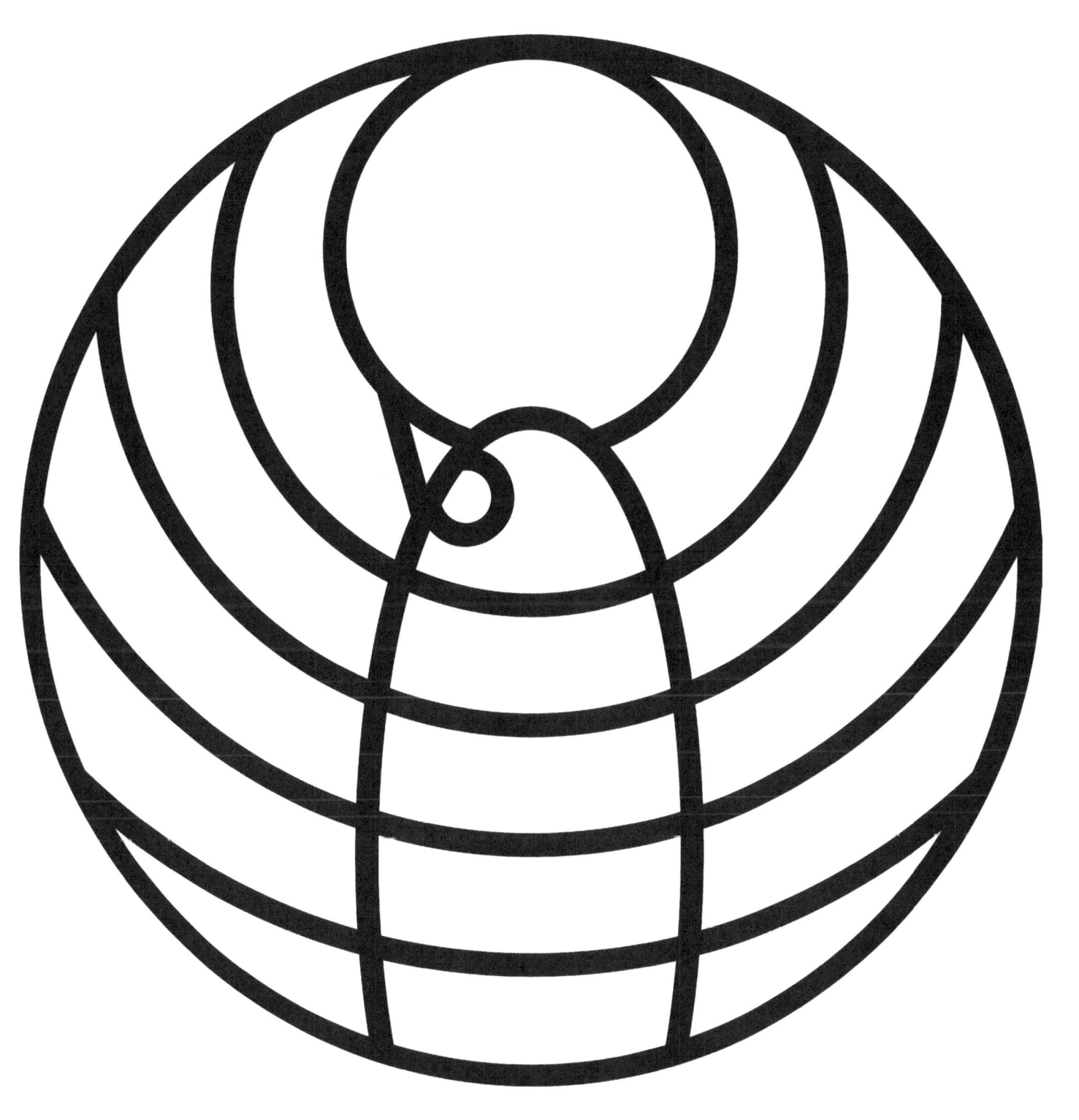

Large Print Adult Coloring Book: Owls and Other Birds

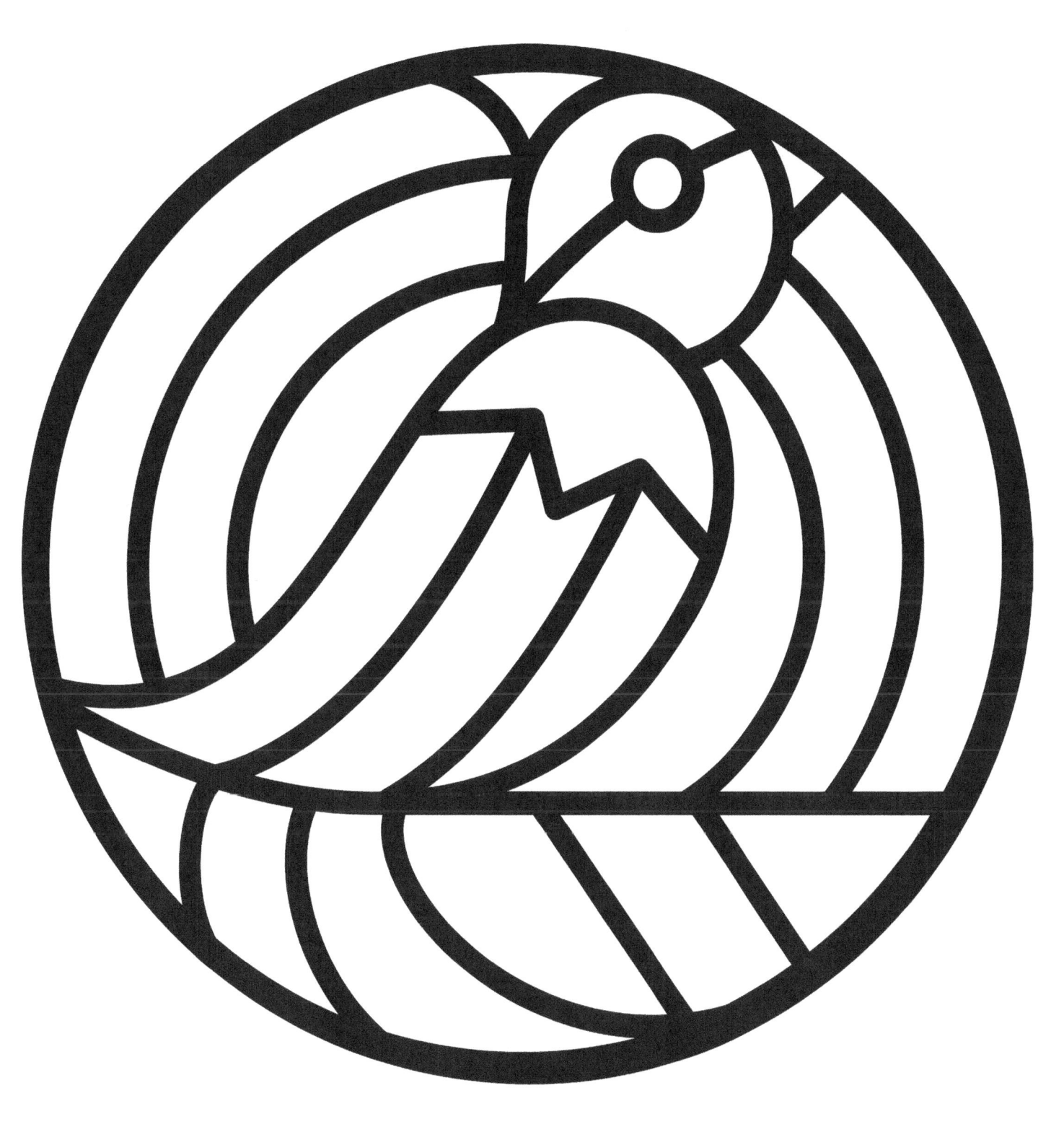

Large Print Adult Coloring Book: Owls and Other Birds

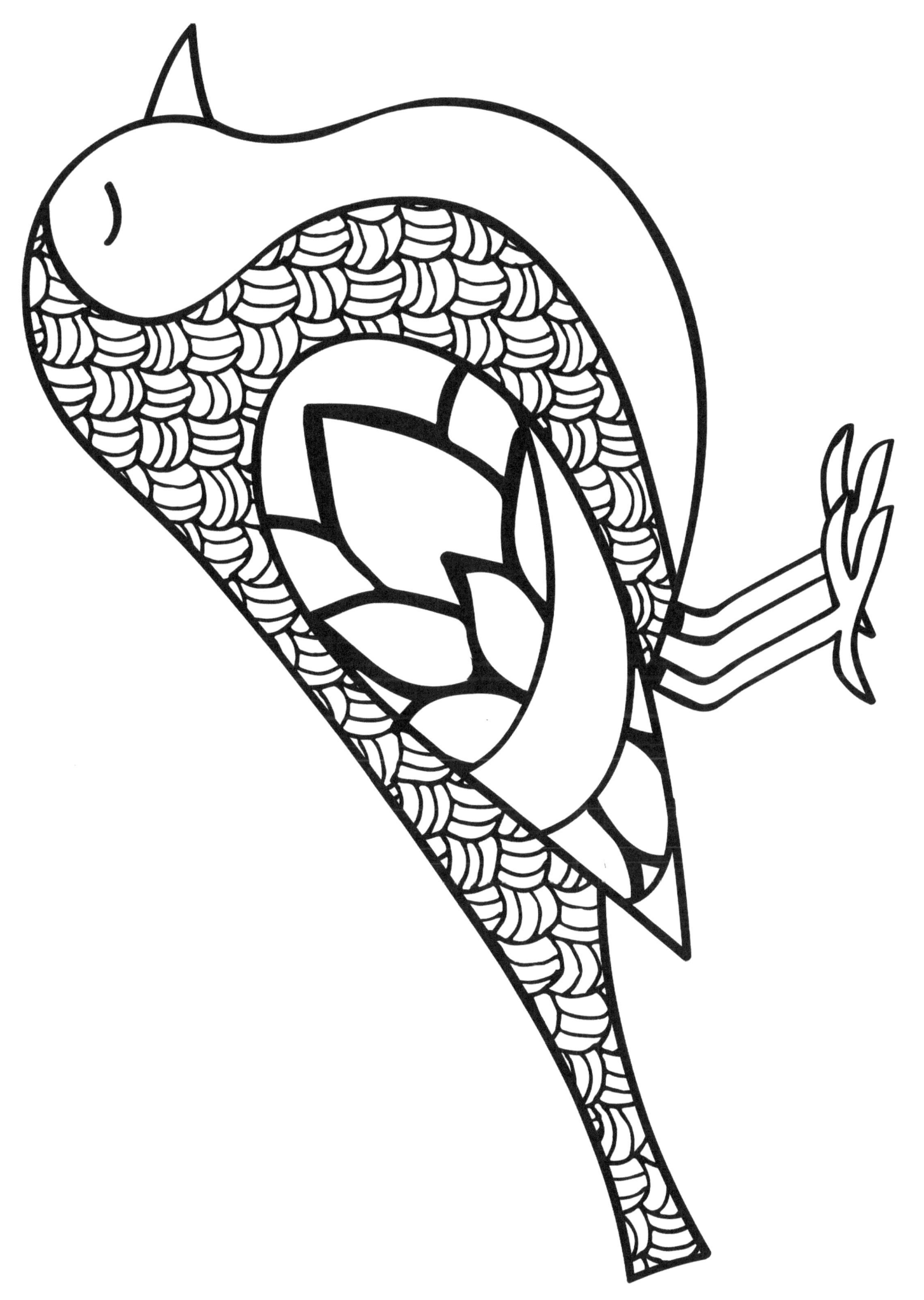

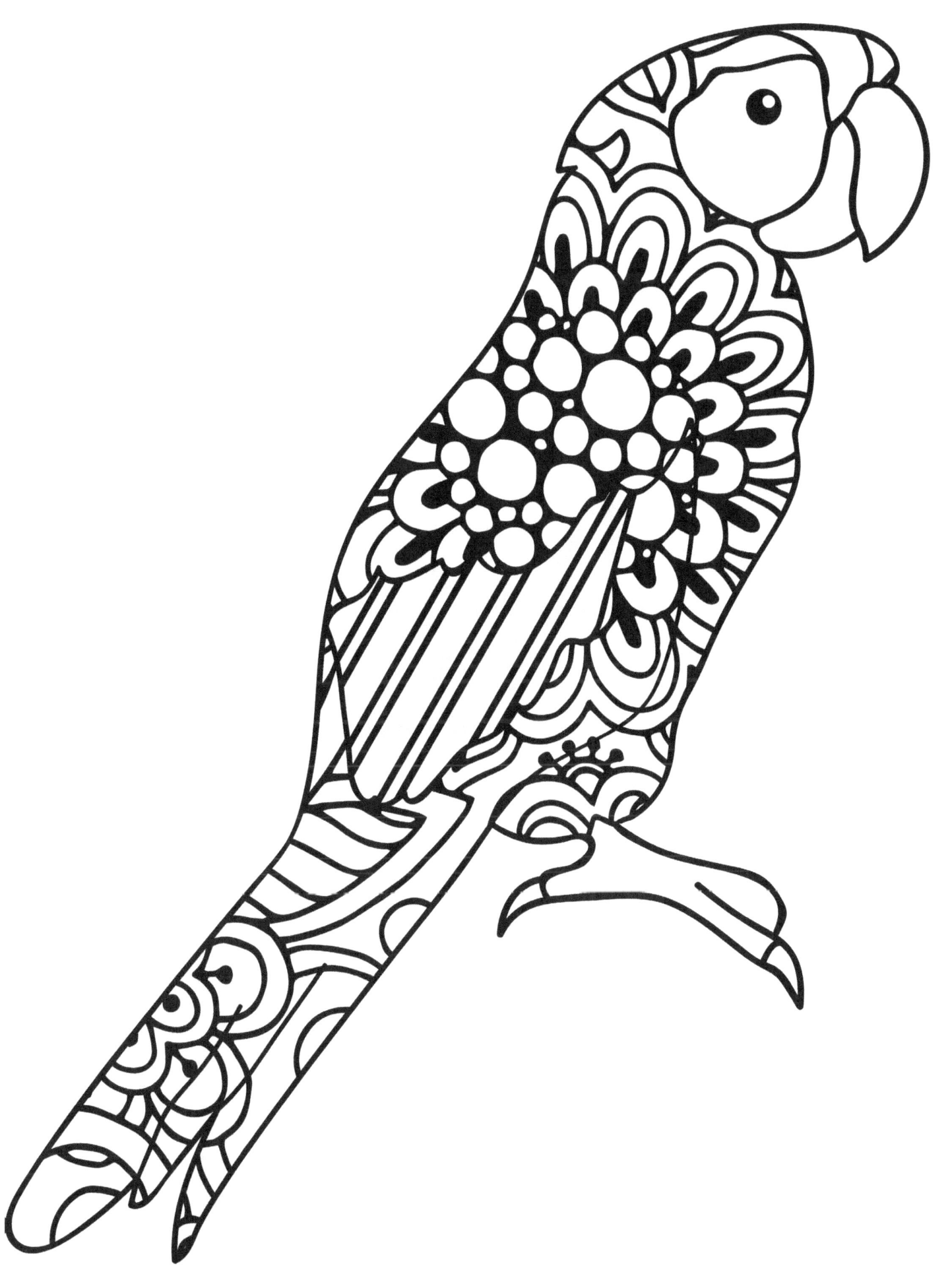

Large Print Adult Coloring Book: Owls and Other Birds

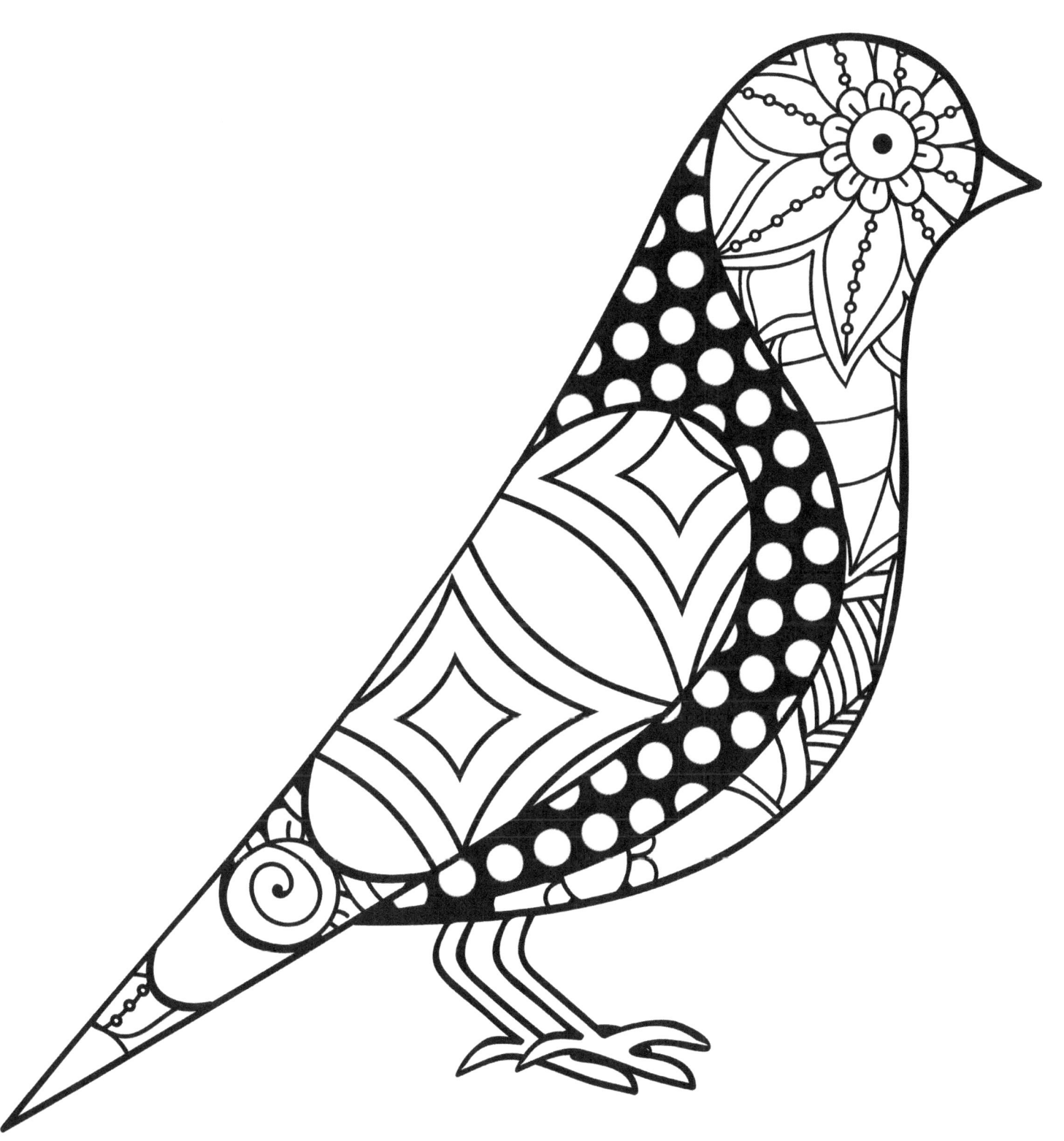

Large Print Adult Coloring Book: Owls and Other Birds

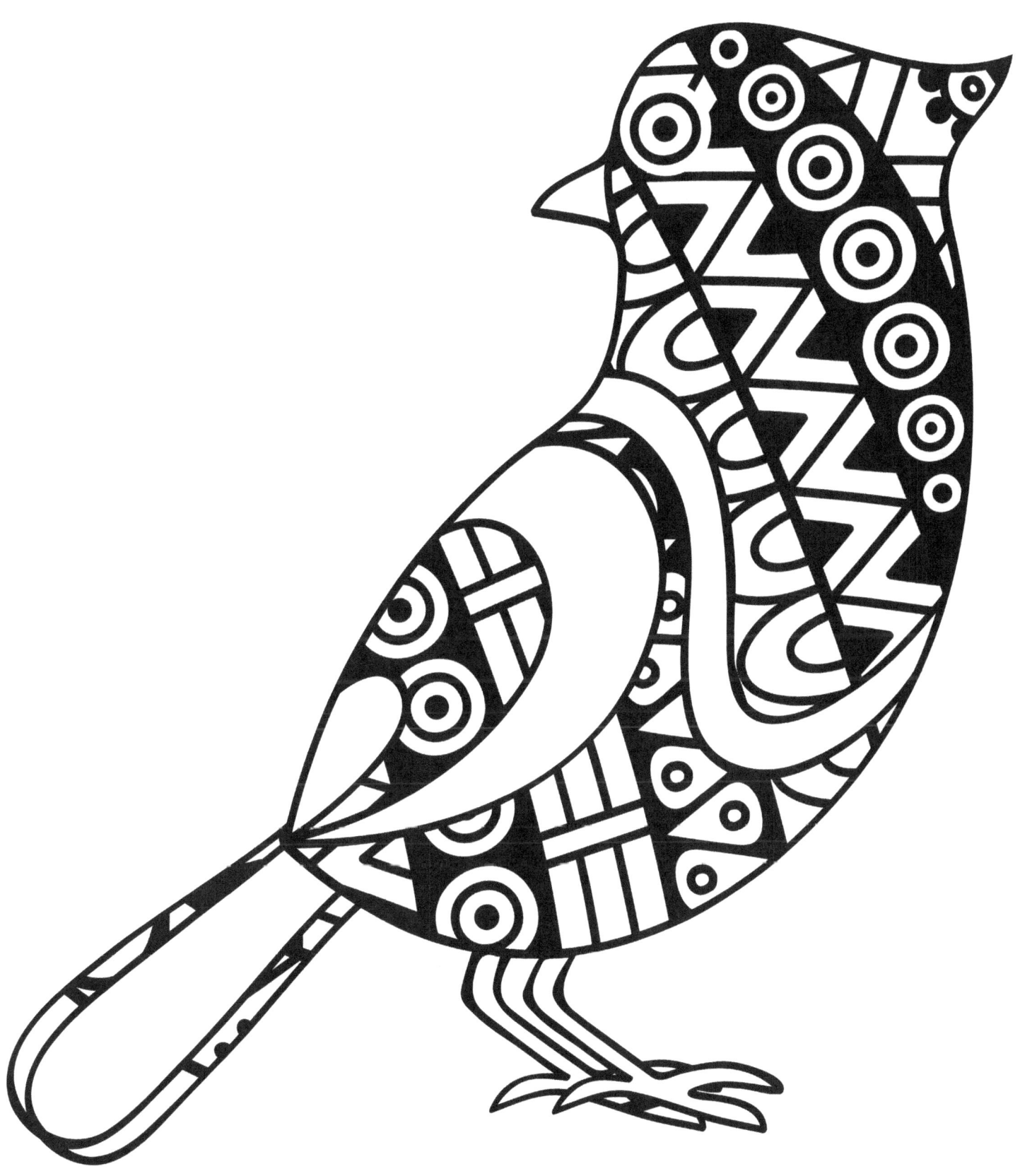

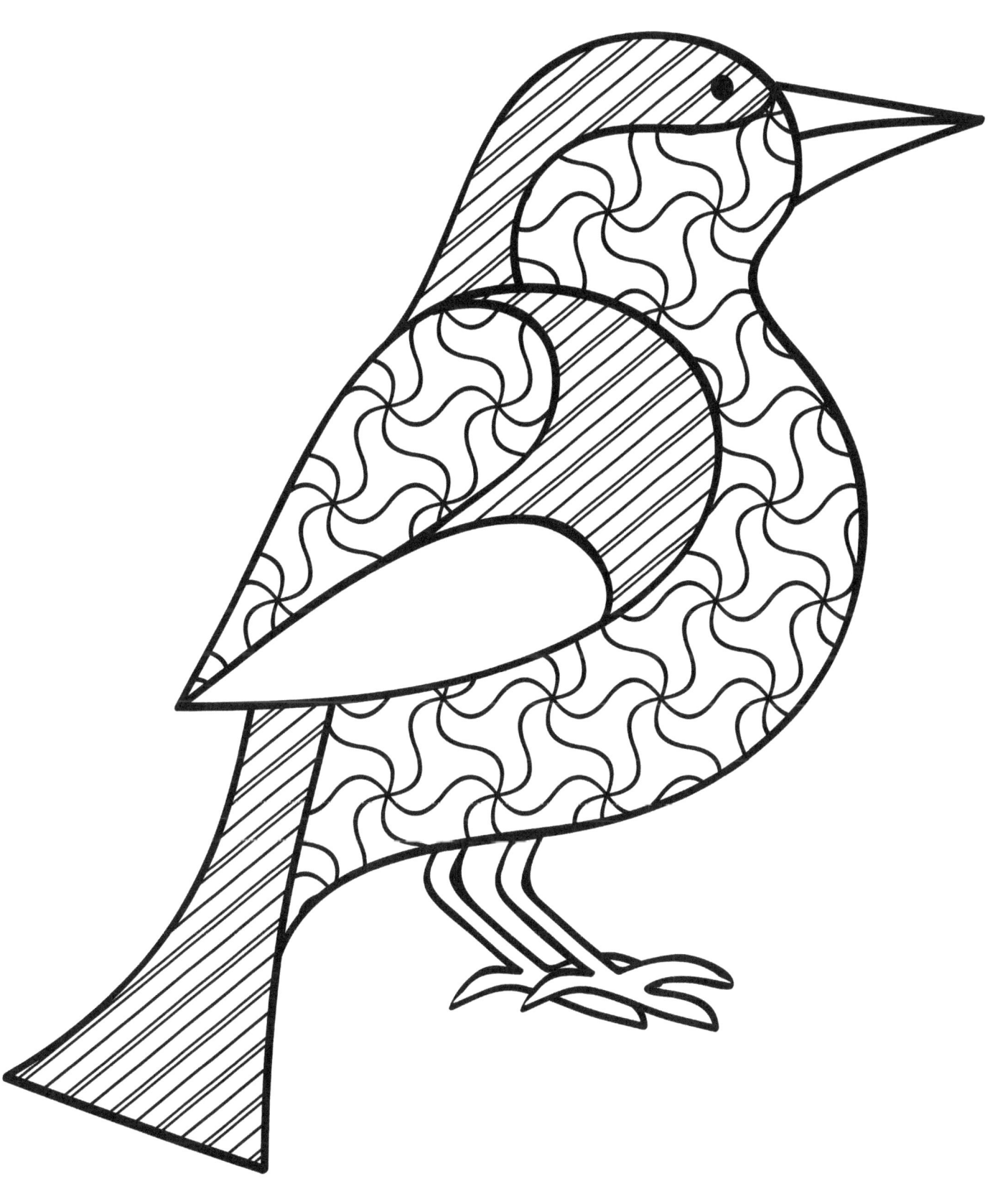

Large Print Adult Coloring Book: Owls and Other Birds

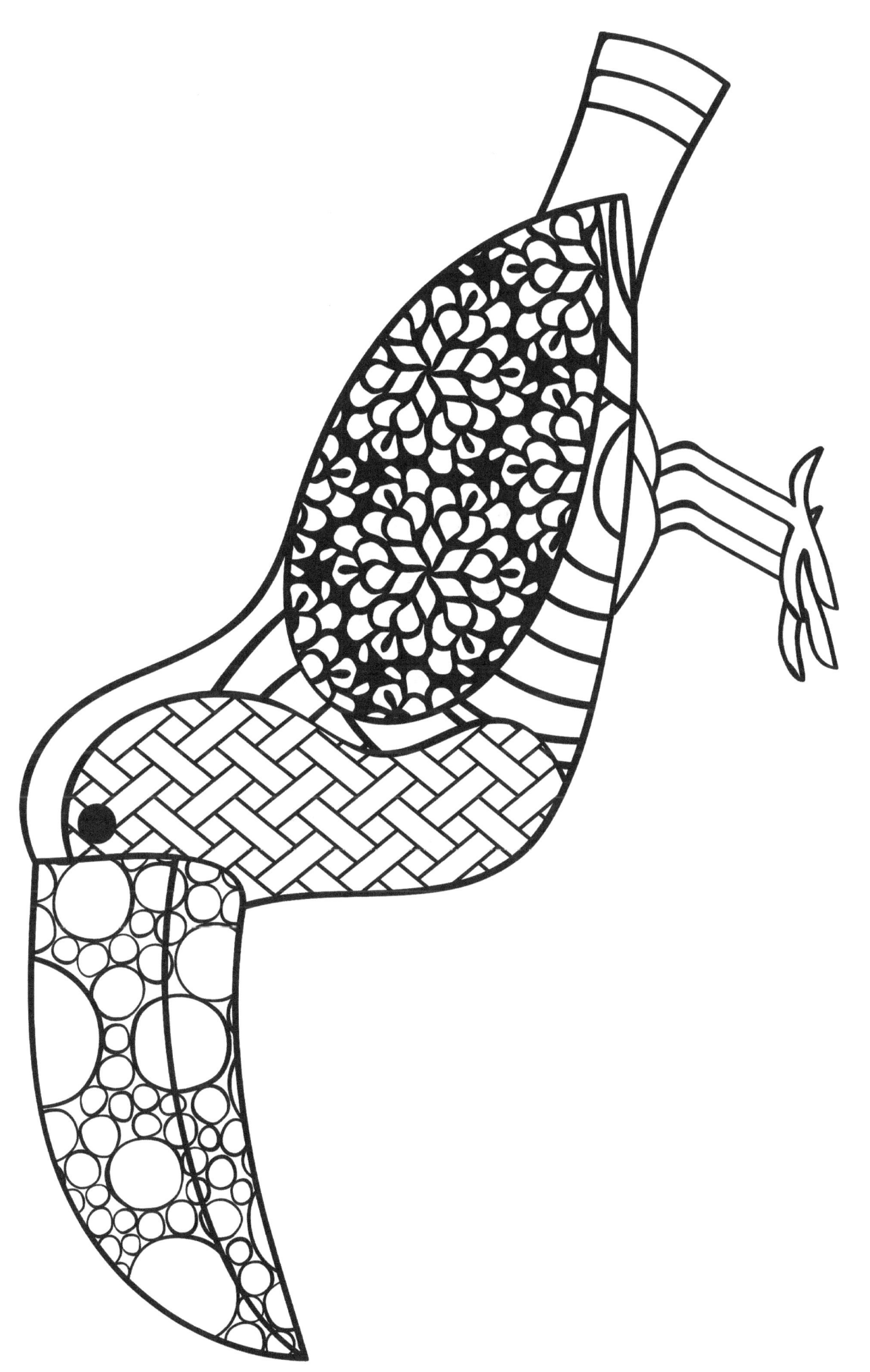

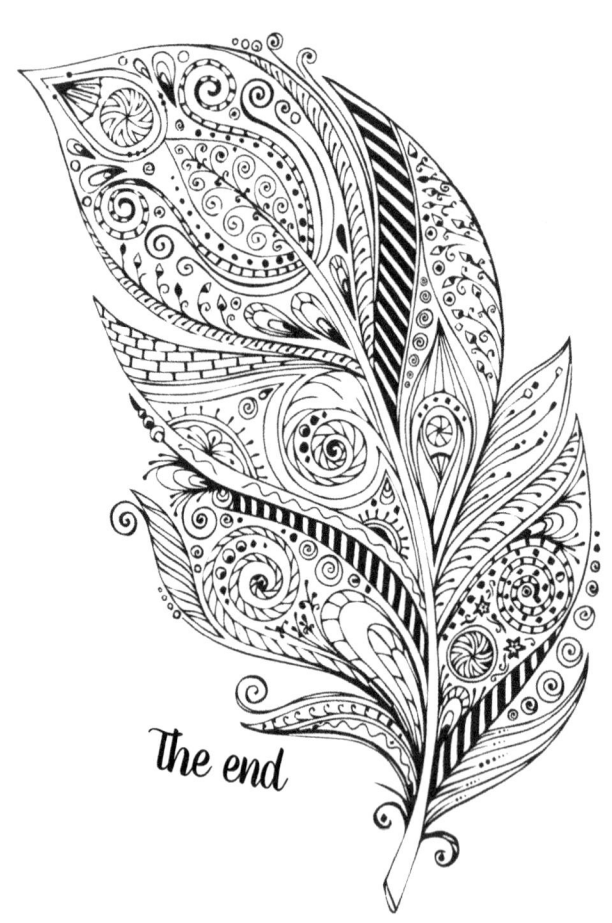

the end

Bonus! Free bookmarks

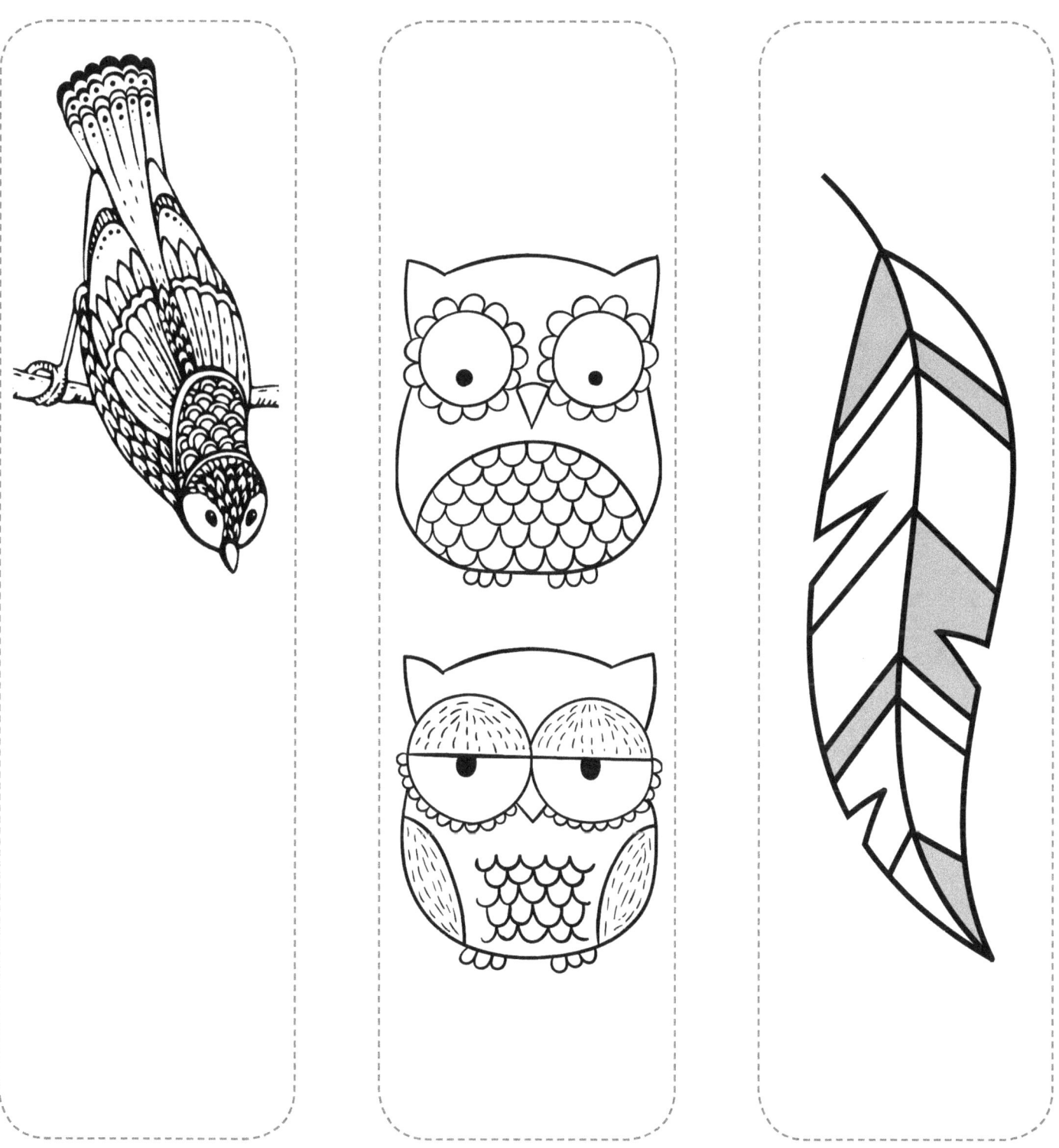

After coloring the images, you can (1) Paste the bookmark on a thick piece of paper and cut it out
on the dotted lines, or (2) Cut it out on the dotted lines and laminate each bookmark.

Like this book? We have others!

Large Print Adult Coloring Book (5 volumes)
Pantsuits: Scrapbook of a Style Revolution
The Beer Lover's Guide to Vintage Advertising
Something Old: Vintage Wedding Dress Fashion Look Book
Motivation & Mandalas Adult Coloring Book: Inspiration for Women
Large Print Word Search Puzzles series (2 volumes)

See the latest and get freebies online at BrilliantActivityBooks.com,
and for more coloring, look for our *Vintage Women: Adult Coloring Book* series!

Other Synchronista titles: *Something Old: Vintage Wedding Dress Fashion Look Book*
All-In-One Pregnancy Calendar, Daily Countdown, Planner & Journal

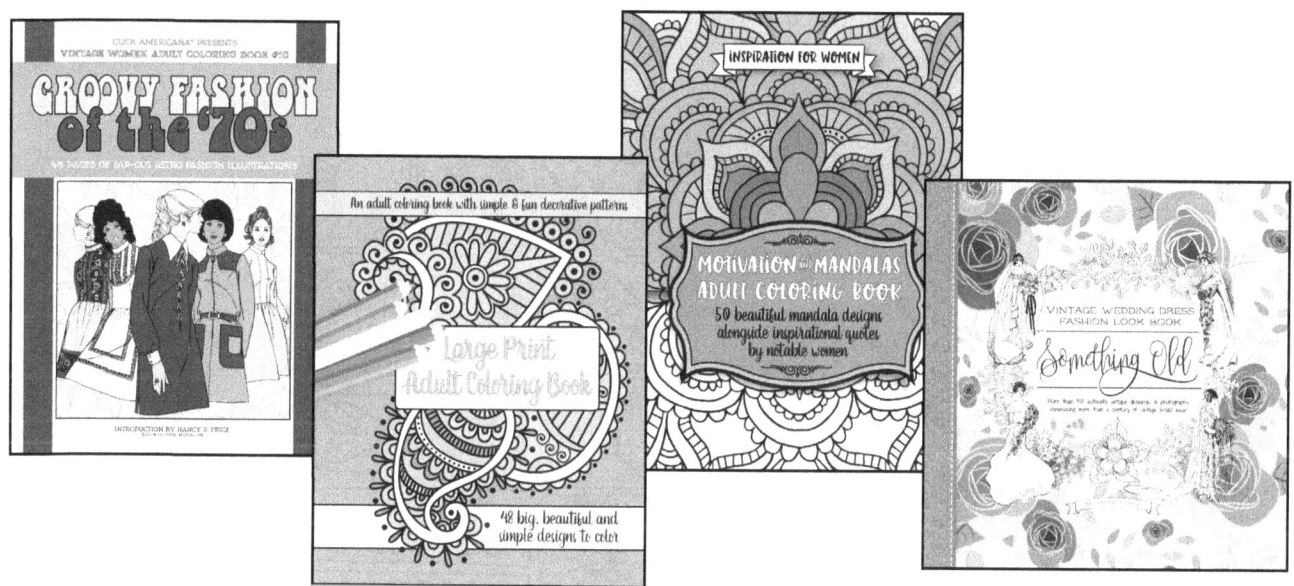

Check out our websites, too...

ClickAmericana.com
Thousands of articles, photos and vintage ads
from throughout American history.

PrintColorFun.com
Hundreds of free coloring pages
to download and print at home.

Myria.com
Smart stuff for real life:
Health, parenting, psychology,
science, tech, entertainment — plus
recipes, home decor & other good things.